P · O · C · K · E · T · S

BIRDS

Written by
BARBARA TAYLOR

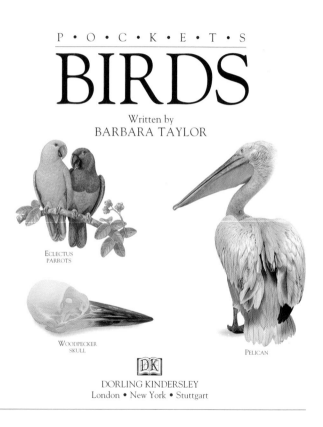

ECLECTUS
PARROTS

WOODPECKER
SKULL

PELICAN

DK

DORLING KINDERSLEY
London • New York • Stuttgart

A DORLING KINDERSLEY BOOK

Project editor Miranda Smith
Senior art editor Helen Senior
Senior editor Susan McKeever
Designer Alexandra Brown
Editorial consultant Peter Colston
Picture research Caroline Brooke
Production Louise Barratt

First published in Great Britain in 1995
by Dorling Kindersley Limited
9 Henrietta Street, Covent Garden, London WC2E 8PS

A CIP catalogue record for this book is available from
the British Library

ISBN 0 7513 5176 8

Colour reproduction by Colourscan, Singapore
Printed and bound in Italy by L.E.G.O.

INTRODUCTION TO BIRDS

P · O · C · K · E · T · S

BIRDS

TAWNY
OWL
FEATHER

EAGLE
OWL
FEATHER

EUROPEAN
EAGLE OWL

CONTENTS

How to use this book 8

HOW TO USE THIS BOOK

These pages show you how to use *Pockets: Birds*.
The book is divided into several sections. The main
section consists of information on birds from different
habitats. There is also an introductory section at the
front, and a reference section at the back. Each new
section begins with a picture page.

HABITATS

The birds in the book are arranged
into habitats. In each habitat
section, you will find information
on the habitat, and examples of
the types of birds that live there.

CORNER CODING

Corners of habitat
pages are colour
coded to remind
you which habitat
section you are in.

 TOWNS, CITIES
AND FARMLAND

FOREST AND
WOODLAND

RAINFORESTS

RIVERS, LAKES,
AND SWAMPS

SEAS, CLIFFS, AND
SHORES

DESERTS, SCRUB,
AND GRASSLANDS

MOUNTAINS AND
MOORLAND

POLAR AND
TUNDRA REGIONS

*Corner
coding*

Heading

Introduction

Caption

RIVERS, LAKES AND SWAMPS

DUCKS

WEBBED FEET and broad, flat bills are a distinctive
feature of ducks. These birds are good swimmers and
strong fliers. There are two main types of duck –
dabbling ducks, such as the mallard,
that feed on the surface, and diving
ducks, such as the pochard. Many
ducks migrate to avoid
cold weather.

DOWN FEATHERS
Female ducks pluck down
feathers from their breasts
and use them to line their
nests and cover the eggs
to keep them warm.

FEMALE

MALE

*Short legs set well
back on body*

MANDARIN DUCKS
These ducks live near ponds
and lakes surrounded by woods, and
nest in tree holes. The male is more
colourful than the female,
except when he moults his
feathers once a year.

HEADING

This describes the
subject of the page.
This page is about
ducks. If a subject
continues over
several pages, the
same heading applies.

INTRODUCTION

This provides a clear,
general overview of the
subject. After reading
this, you should have
an idea what the pages
are about.

CAPTIONS AND
ANNOTATIONS

Each illustration has a
caption. Annotations, in
italics, point out features
of an illustration and
usually have leader lines.

RUNNING HEADS
These remind you which section you are in. The top of the left-hand page gives the section name. The right-hand page gives the subject. The page on ducks is in the Rivers, Lakes, and Swamps section.

FACT BOXES
Many pages have fact boxes. These contain at-a-glance information about the subject. This fact box gives details such as the types of eggs and nests ducks have, and the food they eat.

Size indicator   Running head   Fact box

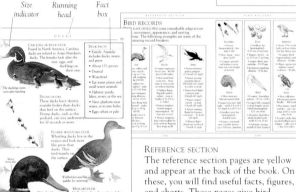

Label   Annotation

REFERENCE SECTION
The reference section pages are yellow and appear at the back of the book. On these, you will find useful facts, figures, and charts. These pages give bird records, such as the biggest and smallest birds, and the fastest flier and runner.

LABELS
For extra clarity, some pictures have labels. They may give extra information, or identify a picture when it is not obvious from the text what it is.

INDEX
There are two indexes at the back of the book – a subject index, and a Latin name index. The subject index lists every subject alphabetically. The Latin name index lists the Latin names of all the birds in the book.

WHAT IS A BIRD?

BIRDS ARE DIFFERENT from all the other animals in
the world because they have feathers – over a
thousand of them. They also have two wings, a
strong bill, no teeth, scaly legs and feet, and three
or four toes with claws on the end. Most birds can
fly, and they are the largest,
fastest, and most powerful flying
animals. Like us, birds breathe
air, have a skeleton inside their
bodies, and are warm-blooded.
Unlike us, birds lay eggs.

JUVENILE
STARLING
FEATHER

ADULT
STARLING
FEATHER

FEATHERS
Birds' feathers are light, yet
strong and flexible. The
feathers of young birds are
often a different colour
from those of the adults.

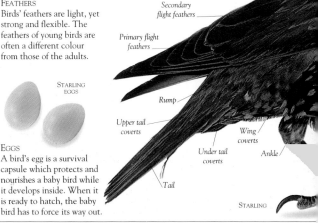

Secondary
flight feathers

Primary flight
feathers

Rump

Upper tail
coverts

Under tail
coverts

Wing
coverts

Ankle

Tail

STARLING
EGGS

EGGS
A bird's egg is a survival
capsule which protects and
nourishes a baby bird while
it develops inside. When it
is ready to hatch, the baby
bird has to force its way out.

STARLING

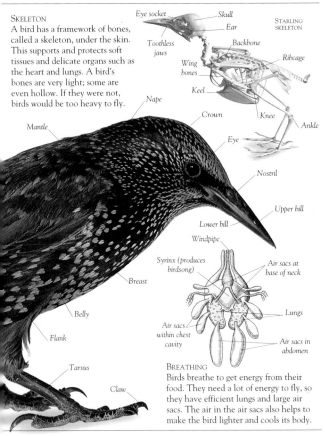

SKELETON

A bird has a framework of bones, called a skeleton, under the skin. This supports and protects soft tissues and delicate organs such as the heart and lungs. A bird's bones are very light; some are even hollow. If they were not, birds would be too heavy to fly.

STARLING SKELETON

Eye socket

Skull

Ear

Toothless jaws

Backbone

Wing bones

Ribcage

Keel

Knee

Ankle

Nape

Crown

Eye

Mantle

Nostril

Upper bill

Lower bill

Windpipe

Syrinx (produces birdsong)

Air sacs at base of neck

Breast

Lungs

Belly

Air sacs within chest cavity

Air sacs in abdomen

Flank

BREATHING

Birds breathe to get energy from their food. They need a lot of energy to fly, so they have efficient lungs and large air sacs. The air in the air sacs also helps to make the bird lighter and cools its body.

Tarsus

Claw

Types of birds

The huge variety of birds alive today – over 9,000 species – evolved from reptile-like creatures that climbed trees about 150 million years ago. Reptile scales developed into bird feathers, although there are still scales on a bird's legs. Now, there are birds of all shapes and sizes, from huge ostriches to tiny wrens. Some of the main types of bird are shown here.

PIGEON

PIGEONS
Most pigeons and doves have rather small heads, plump bodies, dense, soft feathers and a powerful straight flight. They live all over the world.

ARCHAEOPTERYX
The first bird we know of lived about 150 million years ago. It is called *Archaeopteryx*, meaning ancient wing. It could not fly well, but had feathers.

ANCIENT BIRD FACTS
• Birds may be living descendants of the dinosaurs.

• *Archaeopteryx* had teeth.

• The first flying bird was a tern-like seabird called *Ichthyornis*.

• The heaviest bird, *Dromornis stirtoni*, was four times heavier than an ostrich.

ZEBRA FINCHES

PERCHING BIRDS
Over half of the birds alive today are perching land birds. Most are strong fliers and many sing well.

PARROTS
Colourful, noisy, tree-living birds of the tropics, parrots have powerful, hooked bills.

DUCKS
These are broad-bodied water birds with a wide, flat bill, webbed feet, and short legs set well back on the body.

WOOD DUCK

GREEN-WINGED MACAW

KING PENGUIN

GOLDEN EAGLE

PENGUINS
Flightless seabirds of the Southern Hemisphere with wings like flippers.

EAGLES
Powerful birds of prey, eagles have broad, rounded wings, strong talons and a hooked bill.

BLACK-HEADED GULL

GULLS
These stocky seabirds have a heavy bill, long, pointed wings, and webbed feet.

Bird senses

OSTRICH

Birds rely mainly on their eyes and ears to
find food or a mate, to fly, and to escape
from danger. Their eyes are so large that
there is not much room for them to
move in the skull. Instead, birds have
flexible necks and move the
whole head to see things. Most
birds have a poor sense of smell.

SIGHT
A bird's huge eyes are often
as big as its brain. Much of
the brain deals with the
information picked up by the
eyes. Like us, birds see in
colour, but they may have
better eyesight than we have.

*Large eyes
to spot danger
coming*

PIED
AVOCET

*The avocet uses
its sense of touch
to catch small water
creatures.*

TOUCH
Some birds, such as the
avocet, have a well-developed
sense of touch in the tongue
and bill tip. Nightjars have
bristles around their broad bills
to help them sweep moths into
their mouths as they fly at night.

WOODCOCK EYES

To watch for danger, woodcocks have eyes on the side of their head. This helps them to see all around, but there are two blind spots behind and in front of the head.

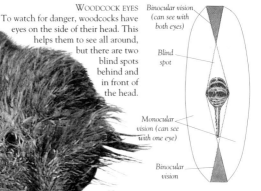

Binocular vision (can see with both eyes)

Blind spot

Monocular vision (can see with one eye)

Binocular vision

HEARING

Birds hear a greater frequency of sound – more sounds per second – than we can. Their ears are hidden under the feathers at the sides of the head. Good hearing is especially important to birds that hunt in the dark.

A bird breathes and smells through two openings in its bill.

BROWN KIWI

SMELL

Most birds seem to have a poor sense of smell, but there are a few exceptions. The kiwi smells food with nostrils at the tip of its long bill. The vultures of the Americas can detect the smell of rotting dead animals from some distance. Some seabirds can pick up scents carried by the wind.

FEATHERS

A BIRD'S BODY is almost completely covered with feathers, although some birds have bare legs. Feathers keep the bird warm, give it shape, colour and pattern, and help some birds to fly. Some birds have special display feathers. Feathers carry out so many important jobs they need to be kept in good condition.

What is a feather?

There are three main types of feather – flight, body, and down. Feathers grow out of pits or follicles in a bird's skin, like the hairs all over our skin. They can be easily repaired because of the way the parts of the feather hook together.

Vane

Smooth, curved shape for flight

Shaft or rachis

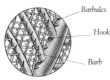

Barbules

Hook

Barb

BARBS AND BARBULES
Each side of a feather consists of parallel barbs, held in place by tiny hooks on side branches called barbules. There are many thousands of barbules on a flight feather.

MACAW FLIGHT FEATHER

FEATHER STRUCTURE
Feathers have a central shaft with a vane or web on either side. They are made of a strong, flexible material called keratin, which also forms our hair and nails.

FLIGHT FEATHERS
Found in the wings and tail, flight feathers provide a large area to push the bird through the air. Their special aerofoil shape lifts the bird in the air, and controls the way it twists and turns in flight.

PEACOCK DOWN FEATHER

Short shaft

REGENT PARROT FLIGHT FEATHERS

DOWN FEATHERS
The soft down feathers trap warm air next to the body and are very important in young birds. The barbs are long and soft and the barbules do not hook together so the feather stays fluffy.

Long shaft

AFRICAN GREY PARROT BODY FEATHER

Inner fluffy part to keep bird warm

Quill

FEATHER FACTS

• Swans have 25,000 feathers, sparrows 3,500, and hummingbirds less than 1,000.

• The male crested argus pheasant has the longest and largest tail feathers at 173 cm (5.7 ft) long, 13 cm (5.1 in) wide.

• Feathers evolved from reptile scales.

• Grebes eat their feathers to help digestion.

BODY FEATHERS
Overlapping like tiles on a roof, body feathers act as a weatherproof jacket. The inner part has softer barbs and the barbules have no hooks.

Feather colour

The colours of bird feathers are produced in two main ways. One is by chemical pigments laid down in the feather when it is being formed. The other is by the structure of feathers and the way they reflect the light. Bird colours help individuals of the same species to recognize each other. They also help birds to attract a mate, threaten a rival, or camouflage themselves.

SHINING COLOURS
Peacock feathers are iridescent – they change colours as they move. This is probably caused by a mixture of pigments and reflection of the light.

Male peacock uses his colourful feathers in a courtship display

FLAMINGO
FEATHERS

FOOD COLOUR
The colour of flamingo feathers comes from a pink pigment in the shrimps and other small water creatures which the birds sieve from the water.

PEACOCK
FEATHERS

LIGHT COLOURS
These macaw feathers
are blue above and
brownish below. This
effect is caused by
the way light is
reflected from them.

MACAW
FEATHERS

*Tropical birds
often have
brightly coloured
feathers.*

PIGMENT COLOURS
This parakeet feather
has red, orange,
yellow and dark
brown colours. The
melanin pigment
produces black and
brown colours.
The carotenoid
pigment causes red,
orange, and yellow.

PARAKEET
FEATHER

Looking after feathers

Birds must take great care of their feathers
and spend a few hours each day cleaning
and tidying their plumage.
They use the bill to
pull ruffled feathers
into shape, and
may also take
water or dust
baths. Many
birds spread
an oily liquid
over their
feathers to
keep them
waterproof.

YELLOW
CANARY
PREENING

PREENING

To preen its feathers, a bird draws
each one carefully through its bill.
This fits the barbs and barbules back
into place – like pulling up a zip – and
cleans and smooths the feathers.
Preening also removes parasites, such
as feather lice, which live on feathers
and eat them.

*Most birds use
their feet to
preen their head
feathers.*

*The oil used for preening
comes from a special
gland at the base of the
tail, on the rump.*

BIRD BATH
Many birds, like the blue tit below, bathe in water. They clean their feathers and skin, and get ready for preening. Most birds bathe and preen regularly. Some also take dust baths, perhaps to get rid of parasites.

NEW FEATHERS
A new feather is rolled up as a cylinder inside a thin, horny sheath. When it is fully developed, the sheath splits open and flakes away. The feather can then unroll and begin to grow to its full length.

Emerging adult feather

Fully grown tail feather

MOULTING KING PENGUINS

Young penguins lose their fluffy feathers

Horny sheath

ADULT KESTREL FEATHER

YOUNG KESTREL FEATHER

GROWING FEATHERS
At least once a year, most birds moult their feathers and new feathers grow to replace old ones. Moulting allows birds to replace worn or damaged feathers, and to change colour as they grow up or the seasons change.

HOW BIRDS MOVE

TO FIND FOOD and escape danger, birds walk, run, hop, swim, and wade. Most birds can also fly. They have light bones, powerful flight muscles, and an efficient respiratory system. A few birds cannot fly. Some of these flightless birds run very fast indeed.

Flight

In order to fly, birds flap their wings up and down. As the wings beat down, they push the air back, and the bird moves forwards. Air flows over and under the wings creating a lifting force.

LIFT
Birds have curved wings made of feathers to push and steer them through the air. The inner part of a bird's wing can stay still to provide lift.

TAKE-OFF
A heavy bird, such as a swan, has to run along while flapping its wings to get enough lift for take-off. Smaller birds take off by jumping into the air and flapping their wings to create lift.

TAWNY OWL

COMING IN TO LAND

To land, birds slow down in mid-air, then drop gently to the ground, onto a perch, or the surface of water, spreading out their wings and tail like brakes. Heavy birds land into the wind to help slow themselves down.

Strong legs to absorb impact of landing

Wings and tail spread to increase air resistance and drag

BLUE-AND-WHITE FLYCATCHER

CURVED WINGS

A bird's wing is an aerofoil shape – curved on top and slightly hollow underneath. The air flows faster over the top, creating low air pressure, while air pressure underneath stays much the same. The difference in pressure produces lift.

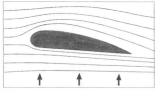

Finger-like feathers to push and steer through the air

MUTE SWAN

Neck stretched out and feet tucked up to streamline bird's body

FLIGHT FACTS

• Common swifts may stay in the air for three years at a time without landing.

• Some hummingbirds beat their wings up to 90 times a second.

• Swans have been recorded flying as high as 8,230 m (27,000 ft).

• Peregrine falcons can reach speeds of 180 km/h (112 mph) when diving after prey.

Flight patterns

Different kinds of bird have differently shaped wings which they flap in patterns that suit their lifestyle. To save energy, some birds like seagulls and vultures soar on rising air, while smaller birds glide between flaps of the wings. Ducks and other heavy birds flap their wings all the time they are in the air. A few, such as hummingbirds and kestrels, can hover in one spot.

Feathers spread apart on upstroke for air to slip through wing

FLIGHT PATH
Small birds, like this minla, have a bouncing, undulating flight. Bigger birds such as cranes, ducks, and geese tend to fly in straight lines.

RED-TAILED MINLA

Eagles thermalling

Hot air rising

Seabirds have powerful flight muscles.

GLIDING IN A THERMAL

GLIDING AND SOARING
Seabirds glide upwards on air currents rising from waves or over cliffs. Large birds of prey, such as eagles or vultures, also use natural currents of rising hot air to lift them higher into the air. These currents are called thermals.

HOVERING
Hummingbirds can hover, move straight up or down, and even fly backwards. They do this by turning each wing in a circle, and using up and down wingbeats for extra power.

HUMMINGBIRD

Unlike other birds, hummingbirds have rigid wings with a swivel joint at the shoulder.

Between flaps, wings fold against body so bird can glide and rest

Feathers closed together on downstroke to push against the air

Tail used for steering and changing direction

GLIDING
HERRING GULL

Long, narrow wings for gliding

Feathers hug the body, creating a streamlined shape so air can flow past more easily

WING SHAPE
The size and shape of wings give clues to how a bird lives and helps with identification, especially if the bird is high in the sky.

Long and wide for soaring – buzzards and vultures

Long and narrow for gliding – fulmars and albatrosses

Wide and rounded for short, fast flight – pheasants

Narrow and pointed for fast flight – swallows and swifts

Flightless birds

CASSOWARY
AND CHICK

A few birds have given up flying altogether. Some of them are so good at swimming or running that they do not need to fly. Many flightless birds, such as ostriches, rheas, or emus are very large birds that can run faster than their enemies, or can win a fight so easily that they do not need to fly away. Some flightless birds live on remote islands where there are few enemies from which they need to escape.

DEFENCE
With powerful legs and dagger-like claws, birds such as cassowaries do not need to fly away. Cassowaries even attack people, lashing out with strong feet and sharp nails.

GALAPAGOS
CORMORANT

FLIGHTLESS FACTS
• The flightless Stephens Island wren was wiped out by a cat within a year of being discovered.

• Ostriches are nearly seven times too heavy to fly. They have the biggest legs of any bird.

• The Inaccessible Island rail is the world's smallest flightless bird, about the size of a chick.

WINGS
Flightless birds usually have small, weak wings which are not strong enough for flight. The Galapagos cormorant uses its wings to help it balance on land.

BIRDS IN DANGER
Many flightless birds, such as this kakapo, are threatened by people who introduce cats and rats to their island homes. Kakapos are too heavy to fly.

KAKAPO

GREATER
RHEA

FAST RUNNERS

Running away from danger can be just as good as flying. Rheas can sprint faster than a horse, reaching speeds of 50 km/h (31 mph), and are also good swimmers. Rheas are related to ostriches and emus and follow a similar lifestyle, but they live on the South American grasslands, rather than on the grasslands of Africa or Australia.

Fluffy wings used for display, not flight

Long neck to see over tall grasses

HUMBOLDT
PENGUIN

FAST SWIMMERS

Penguins are so well suited to their life in the sea that they are a different shape from most birds. They use their wings as flippers for swimming while their feet and tail steer like a rudder.

Large leg muscles provide power when running

Three strong toes on each foot for defence and for running fast

LEGS AND FEET

BIRDS USE their legs and feet for preening their feathers, as well as for moving about. The size and shape of their feet depends on where they live and how they feed.

Three toes point forward and one back

String-like tendons

PERCHING
Birds that perch can sleep without falling off a branch. They bend their legs, pulling the tendons tight and drawing in the toes. This locks their feet tightly round the perch.

TAWNY OWL TALON

TALONS
Birds of prey, such as owls and eagles, have strong, sharp, curved claws called talons. They use these to catch and carry their prey.

Long toes that spread wide

WATTLED JACANA

Scaly skin along each toe

WIDE TOES
Some water birds, such as coots, have lobes of skin on each toe. These push aside the water for faster swimming and help to stop the coot sinking into mud.

COOT TOES

LONG TOES
Jacanas or lily trotters have very long, thin toes. These spread the weight of the bird over a bigger area so it can "trot" across lily pads on the ponds and lakes where it lives.

SPEED
Ostriches have long legs and strong toes to run at speeds of up to 70 km/h (43 mph). They only have two toes on each foot; most birds have three or four.

WEBBED FEET
Water birds, such as ducks, geese, and flamingos have webs of skin between their toes. The webs work like paddles when the bird is in water. They are also useful when the bird is walking on soft, marshy ground.

GRIPPING TOES
The two outer toes of a parrot's foot point backwards, and the two inner toes point forwards. This gives parrots a very powerful grip for climbing through the trees. It also allows them to hold food up to the bill.

BLUE FRONTED PARROT

Two toes forward, two toes back

LEGS OF FLAMINGO

COLLARED
SUNBIRD SIPPING
NECTAR

FOOD AND FEEDING

BIRDS SPEND MUCH of their time
finding food, whether pecking at
berries and nuts, or snapping up fish or
small mammals. They rely mainly on their
eyes and ears to find food, and their bill or
claws to catch it. A few birds steal their food
from other birds. Some birds eat plants; others
eat animals or have a mixed diet.

Hunting and fishing

Meat-eating birds usually catch weak
or unfit prey. They may lie in wait to
ambush their quarry, or chase after it
through air or water. Most of these
birds hunt by day; a few, such as
owls, hunt at night.

GREAT WHITE
PELICAN

GOLDEN
EAGLE

BIRDS OF PREY
Most birds of
prey, such as this
golden eagle, soar
high in the sky to
search for food,
then swoop down to
seize and crush their
prey in their sharp talons.
However,
nine out of ten attacks are unsuccessful
and the prey manages to escape.

*A pelican's bill can
hold more food than
its stomach*

UMBRELLA FISHING
Some birds have developed their own special techniques for catching food. The black heron shades the water with its wings. This cuts out reflections and makes it easier for the bird to see fish.

Great white pelicans eat about 1.2 kg (2 ½ lb) of fish a day

SNAKE HUNTERS
Secretary birds are unusual because they search for their prey on foot. They have tough scales on their legs for protection from the snakes' bites. They pin prey to the ground with sharp claws.

SECRETARY BIRDS

Sharp, hooked bill to pull and tear at food

EGYPTIAN VULTURE

FISHING IN GROUPS
Great white pelicans usually fish in groups. The birds gather in a circle on the water, lifting their wings and plunging their bills into the water to drive the fish into the middle of the circle. Then they scoop up the fish.

USING TOOLS
A few birds use tools to find and deal with their food. Egyptian vultures throw or drop stones on to ostrich eggs to break open the thick shells.

What birds eat

Birds have healthy appetites. They need to eat large amounts of food to give them enough energy to fly, keep warm, build nests, and lay eggs. Some birds eat only one kind of food, while others, such as starlings, crows, and jays eat almost anything. Birds such as vultures eat carcasses, the dead bodies of animals.

HELMET BIRD

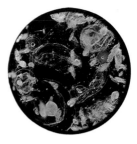

MICROSCOPIC SEAFOOD
A drop of seawater teems with tiny plants such as diatoms and animals such as crab larvae. This plankton floats about the oceans and is a vital part of the diet of many seabirds.

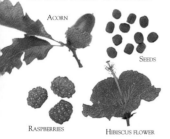

ACORN

SEEDS

RASPBERRIES

HIBISCUS FLOWER

FLOWERS, FRUITS, AND SEEDS
The sweet liquid called nectar produced by flowers is a high-energy food for birds such as hummingbirds. Many birds eat the fruits and seeds that develop when the flowers are pollinated.

GRASS

CABBAGE LEAF

CONIFER

GRASS AND LEAVES
A few birds, such as geese, ducks, and grouse, eat grass and leaves. These can be hard to digest and poor in nutrients, so the birds have to eat a lot of this sort of food to get the energy they need.

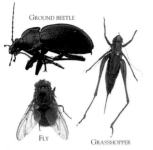

GROUND BEETLE

GRASSHOPPER

FLY

CRAB

SNAIL

COCKLE

EARTHWORM

INSECTS
Adult insects are more abundant in warmer weather, but caterpillars and grubs survive colder periods buried in soil or under bark. Insects are a body-building food, vital for young birds.

INVERTEBRATES
Invertebrates such as crabs and shellfish are an important source of food on the seashore, where there are few insects. Garden and woodland birds, such as thrushes, eat juicy earthworms.

COMMON FROG

VOLE

GRASS CARP

NEST AND YOUNG

VERTEBRATES
Birds that feed on vertebrates (animals with backbones) have to work hard for their meals. The animals they hunt do their best to run, swim or slither away, and often succeed in escaping.

EGGS AND YOUNG
Some birds eat the eggs and helpless young of other birds. For example, skuas pounce on puffin and penguin chicks, and magpies often take eggs and young birds from the nest.

Bird bills

A bird uses its bill like a hand to carry out all sorts of tasks, from catching and holding food to preening its feathers and building a nest. Parrots also use their bills to help them climb. The size and shape of a bird's bill depends mainly on what it eats and where it finds its food.

YELLOW-HEADED PARROT

FRUIT-AND-NUT EATERS
A parrot's bill deals with two different kinds of food. The hook at the tip pulls out the soft parts of fruit, while the strong nutcracker at the base opens seeds. Parrots use their feet to hold food.

FLAMINGO

A flamingo dips its bill upside down in the shallow water.

FILTER-FEEDER
The flamingo has a very special bill. Sievelike edges on the top bill filter out tiny plants, shrimps, and other invertebrates from the water. The bottom bill and the tongue move up and down to pump water through comb-like fringes on the sides of the top bill.

Bee-eaters beat stinging insects against a branch to get rid of the stings.

WHITE-THROATED BEE-EATER

INSECT EATERS
Birds that feed on insects have thin, pointed bills to probe under bark and stones. Birds that eat flying insects have wide, gaping bills to scoop them up as they fly.

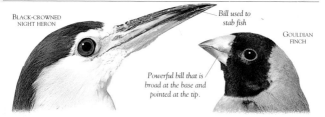

BLACK-CROWNED
NIGHT HERON

*Bill used to
stab fish*

GOULDIAN
FINCH

*Powerful bill that is
broad at the base and
pointed at the tip*

FISH EATERS
A dagger-shaped bill is characteristic of
fish-eating birds, such as herons. Others,
such as cormorants, have a hooked bill
with which to tear the fish into pieces.

SEED EATERS
To crack open seeds, seed-eating birds
such as finches have pyramid-shaped
bills. The hawfinch's bill is so strong it
can even crush cherry stones.

SCARLET-CHESTED
SUNBIRD

*Flaps over
nostrils keep out
flower pollen*

NECTAR EATERS
Nearly one-fifth of all the
world's birds feed on nectar.
Sunbirds and hummingbirds
push their needle-like bills into
flowers and lick up the sweet nectar.

*Powerful
hooked bill to
tear up food*

GOLDEN
EAGLE

MEAT EATERS
Often called birds of prey, these include
eagles, owls, and falcons. They use their
bills to pull apart animals they kill into
bite-sized chunks. Owls swallow small
animals, such as voles and mice, whole.

COURTSHIP

BEFORE MATING, male birds usually court the females. Some males grow more colourful or elaborate feathers for the breeding season. They may give singing or dancing displays. Some show off nest-building or hunting skills.

YELLOW-THROATED LAUGHING THRUSH

Laughing thrushes make loud, cackling sounds.

TERRITORY
Many birds nest in an area, or territory, that has enough food for their young when they hatch out. Male birds sing in their territory to attract a mate and keep away other males.

MALE PIN-TAILED WHYDAH

Female bird duller, with short tail

MALES AND FEMALES
Male and female birds of the same species often look different. The male is usually more colourful, but the dull colours of the female help camouflage her on the nest.

Long tail feathers used in display flight to impress females

FEMALE PIN-TAILED WHYDAH

MALE
PEACOCK

*Male's long
feathers make
flight difficult*

DISPLAY
The male
peacock spreads
out his long, colourful
feathers in a shimmering
fan to impress a female.
After the breeding season, the
long tail feathers fall out.

RED-CROWNED
CRANES

*The "eyes"
may hypnotize
the female.*

DANCING
Some birds dance together
before they mate. Cranes jump
up and down in the air with
their partners. Great crested
grebes perform a series of
dances, including head-shaking.

NESTS AND EGGS

ALL BIRDS LAY EGGS and most build nests to keep eggs and young safe and warm. Birds know instinctively how to build a nest, and female birds usually do most of the work. Nests vary from a shallow scrape in the ground and simple cup shapes, to more elaborate constructions.

WAGTAIL NEST

Building a nest

NEST BOX

Birds use a wide range of nesting materials and may make hundreds of trips to collect material. Nest materials must both support the nest and keep the young warm. Nest boxes encourage birds to nest in gardens or woods with few natural tree holes.

PEBBLE NEST
Oystercatchers lay their eggs in a shallow dip, or scrape, on the shoreline. Their eggs are difficult to see among the pebbles.

TWIGS
Most hedgerow and woodland birds use twigs and sticks to support their nests as these are readily available.

FEATHERS
Birds may use feathers as a warm lining for a nest. Hundreds of feathers line a long-tailed tit's nest.

To make the cup shape, birds turn round and round.

MOSS

Moss traps warm air in the nest and stops heat loss. It helps to keep both eggs and young birds warm.

Woodpeckers have chisel-like bills.

STRING

Birds sometimes collect household materials when nest-building. Pieces of string have been found in many nests.

TREE NEST

Woodpeckers dig nest holes in rotten trees with their strong beaks. Many other birds use existing tree holes. The nests inside the holes are usually lined with grass or feathers.

MUD

Some nests are lined with wet mud mixed with saliva and droppings. When it dries, it forms a hard and strong lining.

GRASS

Grass is a flexible nest material. It is used by many birds because it is easy to weave into differently shaped nests.

MUD NEST

Swallows and martins collect mud with their bills and build nests with pieces of mud stuck together with saliva.

HOUSE MARTIN NEST

41

Unusual nests

From woven purses and saliva cups to mud
ovens and compost heaps, some birds' nests
are quite unusual and elaborate. They may
be a strange shape, such as the trumpet-
like weaver bird nests. Birds need a lot of
practice to perfect
the technique of
making a
complex
nest.

PENDULINE
TIT NEST

*Strong and
lightweight
basket*

*False
entrance*

WOVEN NEST
A male West African weaver
bird knotted grasses to weave
this nest. The entrance
tunnel stops snakes and other
enemies from getting inside.

PURSE NEST
The penduline tit weaves a
hanging nest from grasses,
leaves, and moss. A false
entrance leads to an empty
chamber and dead end.

THATCHED COTTAGE
Each colony of the
sociable weaver bird of
South Africa builds a
huge "haystack" that is
up to 4 m (13 ft) deep
and 7.2 m (24 ft)
across. Up to 300 pairs
then build their nests
under the protection
of this thatched roof.

WEAVER
NEST

4 2

NEST FACTS

• Biggest nest ever found: a bald eagle's which was 2.9 m (9.5 ft) wide and 6 m (20 ft) deep.

• A bee hummingbird's nest is no bigger than a thimble.

• A mallee fowl's nest is a "compost heap" of rotting vegetation.

• A hammerkop nest may be made of over 10,000 sticks.

BASKET NEST

Reed warblers join their nest to several reed stems. This helps to hold the nest steady as the wind blows. The nest is made from grass, reed fibres, and feathers.

Nest is joined to reeds

TAILOR BIRD ON NEST

REED WARBLER NEST

SEWING BIRD

The tailorbird sews a pocket of leaves to support its nest. Its sharp bill makes a row of holes along the edges of the leaves. Then the bird pulls spider or insect silk or plant material through the holes to stitch the leaves.

STRING NEST

Many birds that nest near people make use of artificial materials. This Baltimore oriole has used pieces of string in its bag-like nest, and has even joined the nest to a twig with string.

All kinds of eggs

Birds lay eggs because they would be too heavy to fly if they carried their young around inside them. Some birds lay one large clutch (set of eggs) in a season, while others lay several smaller clutches. Birds such as snowy owls lay extra clutches if there is plenty of food. No two eggs have exactly the same markings. The colour and shape depends on where the eggs are laid and how much camouflage they need.

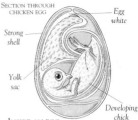

SECTION THROUGH CHICKEN EGG

Egg white

Strong shell

Yolk sac

Developing chick

INSIDE AN EGG
A bird's egg contains a developing bird – an embryo – plus a store of food and a supply of air. Pores in the shell allow air to pass through from outside. The egg white supplies proteins, water, and vitamins.

EGG FACTS

• One ostrich egg has the same volume as 24 hens' eggs.

• Cuckoos can lay eggs in a few seconds; some birds take 1-3 minutes.

• Nearly 80 species of bird lay eggs in the nests of other species.

• Grey partridges lay the largest clutches – up to 16 eggs.

• Most small eggs take under an hour to hatch.

BARN OWL EGG

CURLEW EGG

WHITE EGGS
Birds that nest in holes or burrows, such as owls or kingfishers, usually lay white eggs. They do not need to be camouflaged because they are hidden.

SPECKLED EGGS
Birds that nest in the open, where there is little cover, usually lay patterned eggs. The camouflage colours hide the eggs from enemies.

PALE EGG

SPECKLED EGG

DARK EGG

DISGUISE
Female cuckoos lay their eggs in the nests of other birds such as dunnocks, robins, wrens, or meadow pipits. The foster parents raise the cuckoo chick as their own. The cuckoo's egg often looks similar to those of the foster parents.

COLOURS IN A CLUTCH
The three eggs above were laid by a single snipe but come from different clutches. In one clutch, the eggs usually look similar.

CUCKOO EGG

GUILEMOT EGG

EURASIAN ROBIN EGGS

BIG AND SMALL
Ostriches lay the largest eggs of any living bird. Each egg weighs about 1.7 kg (3.7 lb), and is as long as an adult human's hand. Hummingbirds' eggs, however, are only as big as peas.

HUMMINGBIRD EGGS

OSTRICH EGG

PATTERNS
Common guilemot eggs show a variety of patterns and colours, possibly to help parent birds recognize them. The pear shape stops it rolling off cliff ledges.

BIRTH AND GROWTH

PARENT BIRDS SIT on their eggs to keep them warm so that the chicks inside can develop properly. This is called incubation. After hatching, the parents work hard feeding the chicks, keeping them warm and clean, and protecting them from enemies.

Egg to chick

Most birds develop patches of bare skin, brood patches, to let body warmth through to the eggs they are incubating. Small birds incubate eggs for about two weeks, eagles for six or seven weeks, and albatrosses for up to 11 weeks.

SWAN INCUBATING EGGS IN NEST

First the chick pecks at shell to make a hole

Then chick cuts a circle

Chick pushes to widen crack

HATCHING
To break out of its shell, a baby bird chips away with a pointed "egg tooth" on top of its bill. This egg tooth disappears soon after hatching. Some clutches hatch together; others hatch at intervals of a few day.

Helpless young are usually born in a nest.

BLUE TIT NEST

HELPLESS CHICKS
Birds born naked, blind, and feeble are called altricial. They grow at a very fast rate, often eating their own weight in a day. Songbirds, such as thrushes and chaffinches, are born like this.

INDEPENDENT CHICKS
Some chicks are born with feathers, and are able to see and run soon after hatching. They are called precocial. Ducks, geese, and quails are born like this.

Wet and bedraggled chick struggles free

Dry and fluffy feathers

BLUE-SCALED QUAIL CHICK

Growing up

Baby birds take a few weeks or a few months to grow up. They all rely on their parents to keep them warm and out of danger, and most chicks are fed by their parents as well. Small birds can make hundreds of feeding trips in a day; larger birds only two or three. Chicks that are born helpless grow faster than chicks that are born fluffy and alert.

EAGLE AND CHICKS

HEN AND CHICKS

BIRDS OF PREY
Eagles and other birds of prey tear up food for their chicks at first. As the chicks grow bigger, they learn to do this for themselves.

INDEPENDENT FEEDERS
Some baby birds, such as chickens, ducks, and geese, can feed themselves soon after hatching. At first, they peck at anything; then they watch their parents to find out what to eat.

PECKING SPOT
A herring gull chick pecks at a red spot on its parent's bill to make the parent cough up food. Herring gulls feed out at sea, so they swallow food to help them carry it long distances.

HERRING GULL

CRECHE OF YOUNG
KING PENGUINS

SAFETY IN NUMBERS
Young penguins cannot join their
parents in the water until they
have grown waterproof adult
feathers. The parent birds leave
them behind when they go to
sea to feed. When they
return, the adults cough up
partly digested fish for the
chicks, but there may be a
wait of days or even
weeks between meals.

*Young penguins huddle
together for warmth and
protection while their
parents are away.*

JUVENILE
STARLING

*A young starling
takes off unsteadily
for its first flight*

FIRST FLIGHT
Baby birds have to learn how to fly
as quickly as possible to avoid
predators and other dangers. They
flap their wings while they are in the
nest to exercise their muscles, and make
them strong. Taking off and landing is
not easy – many young birds crash-land.

MIGRATION

NEARLY HALF the world's birds migrate – to find food and water, to nest, or to avoid bad weather. They navigate by instinct, but use familiar landmarks, the Sun, the Moon, the stars, and the Earth's magnetic field to find their way. Migration journeys are often dangerous for birds and use up a lot of energy. Some small birds double their weight to provide enough fuel for travelling.

RED-BREASTED
GOOSE

NESTING
This goose is one of many birds that migrate to the Arctic tundra to nest in the brief summer when there is plenty of food available.

MIGRATION ROUTES

ARCTIC TERN
This is the champion bird migrant, flying from the Arctic to Antarctica and back each year. It spends summer in both polar regions.

AMERICAN GOLDEN PLOVER
This plover has the longest migration of all land birds. It breeds in northern Canada and flies to the Argentinian pampas for the winter.

V-FORMATION

Flying in a V-shaped formation helps birds to save energy on a long journey. The birds following the leader fly in the "slipstream" of the bird in front. When the leader tires, another bird takes over.

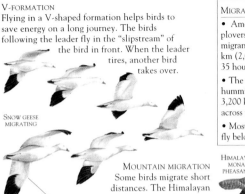

SNOW GEESE MIGRATING

Snow geese breed in the Arctic tundra and migrate to the Gulf of Mexico for the winter.

MIGRATION FACTS

• American golden plovers are fast migrants flying 3,300 km (2,050 miles) in 35 hours.

• The ruby-throated hummingbird travels 3,200 km (2,000 miles) across the Americas

• Most migrating birds fly below 91 m (300 ft).

MOUNTAIN MIGRATION

Some birds migrate short distances. The Himalayan monal pheasant migrates up and down the mountains with the seasons, moving to warmer, lower slopes in winter.

HIMALAYAN MONAL PHEASANTS

SHORT-TAILED SHEARWATER

Between breeding seasons off southern Australia, this bird flies in a figure-of-eight route from Australia to the North Pacific and back again.

WHITETHROAT

This small warbler breeds in Europe in spring and summer, and then migrates to Africa just south of the Sahara Desert for the winter.

WHERE BIRDS LIVE

FROM BUSY CITIES to frozen polar regions, birds have adapted to a range of habitats on every continent. Where birds live depends on the food they eat and their nesting requirements, as well as their competitors and predators. In many parts of the world, where people live has had a destructive influence on the distribution of birds.

SEAS, CLIFFS, AND SHORES
Marine habitats are a huge feeding ground for many birds. They nest on shores around all continents.

DESERTS, SCRUB, AND GRASSLANDS
These dry, mainly hot habitats provide little shelter for birds. Food and water may be hard to find.

NORTH AMERICA

SOUTH AMERICA

POLAR AND TUNDRA REGIONS
In the Antarctic, Arctic, and tundra, it is cold and windy. Birds breed there in summer.

RIVERS, LAKES, AND SWAMPS
Lakes and rivers are fresh water, while marshes and swamps are fresh or salt water.

FOREST AND WOODLAND
Conifers and broadleaved trees grow in temperate climates where there is usually rain all year.

TOWNS, CITIES, AND FARMLAND
Birds that have adapted to live near people can take advantage of the extra food and the less severe climate.

MOUNTAINS AND MOORLAND
Moorlands occur in cool, wet uplands. Mountains have a variety of habitats.

RAINFORESTS
These are mostly hot, wet habitats near the Equator in the Americas, Africa, Southeast Asia and northeastern Australia.

TOWNS, CITIES, AND FARMLAND

ABOUT THE HABITAT

BIRDS THAT HAVE LEARNED to live close to people can feast on the food we give them, or the rubbish we throw away, as well as the weeds, flowers, insects, or farm crops around our homes. Buildings, parks, wasteground, meadows, orchards, and hedgerows provide a variety of nesting places for birds.

KESTREL

HUNTING BIRDS
Most birds of prey do not like living near people, but kestrels and sparrowhawks hunt along roadsides and in parks.

HABITAT FACTS
• At night, a city is as much as 5°C (9°F) warmer than the surrounding countryside.

• Some starling roosts in cities may contain over one million birds.

• Only one in ten birds caught in the wild reaches the pet shop alive.

• The African red-billed quelea is the world's worst agricultural bird pest.

CITY BIRDS
Birds such as geese fly over cities on migration routes, or land to feed and roost in city parks. Starlings roost in city centres at night because it is warmer than the countryside.

CAGED BIRDS
Many people keep birds such as budgerigars, canaries, and parrots in cages. They like their colours, their company, and their songs. People breed birds to create colours never seen in the wild.

BLUE BUDGERIGAR

BARN
SWALLOW
FEEDING
YOUNG

NESTS IN BUILDINGS

Window ledges, attics,
barns and even chimney
pots make ideal nesting places for
birds used to nesting on cliffs, rocky
hillsides or trees. Swallows used to
nest in caves, but now many nest
inside buildings.

NESTS IN HEDGEROWS

Hedgerows are small strips of
woodland where birds such as
the song thrush can nest safely.
Birds roost and feed in hedgerows.
They are an important refuge in
open areas of crops and grass.

SONG THRUSH

SONG THRUSH NEST

HOMES AND STREETS

MANY BIRDS HAVE LOST their natural fear of people and live near our homes and in our cities, despite all the noise and pollution. These urban birds change their diet or the places they nest to take advantage of our leftover food scraps, the artificial habitats we build, and the warm climates we create.

HOUSE SPARROW
By following people from country to country, the fearless house sparrow has spread from Europe and Asia over about two-thirds of the world's land surface. It nests in buildings close to people.

The male has a grey crown and black bib.

The house sparrow is friendly and intelligent.

BIRDS IN DANGER
Thousands of birds are taken from the wild every year. This has reduced numbers of some wild birds, especially parrots.

WHITE STORKS
In many parts of Europe, white storks are believed to bring good luck. They often nest on roofs and people may put up platforms to encourage them.

Upright black crest and red streak below eye

HOUSE CROW

The aggressive house crow is always ready to grasp a tasty morsel of food. It lives near busy towns and small villages in India, as well as in other parts of Asia, often swarming in large, busy groups.

Likes to perch on a high branch to sing

RED-EARED BULBUL

The inquisitive red-eared bulbul is not frightened of people and is a common species around the villages of Asia. It has a pleasant and varied song and is often kept as a pet.

Pigeons are tame enough to be fed by hand.

PIGEON

The city pigeons of today are descended from the wild rock doves which people originally kept for food and, later, for racing. Pigeons have a strong muscular part of the stomach called a gizzard to help them grind up seeds.

City pigeons even travel on underground trains.

PARKS AND GARDENS

FROM TREES AND FLOWERBEDS to grassy lawns and garden ponds, parks and gardens contain a great variety of habitats for birds. People put up feeding tables, bird baths, and nesting boxes to encourage birds to live near houses. Unfortunately, pets such as cats often catch and kill garden birds.

BLACK-BILLED MAGPIE
This adaptable magpie visits suburban gardens. It eats a range of food, especially insects and small rodents, but also steals eggs and young from the nests of other birds.

Pale grey border

Red breast and face typical of robins

EURASIAN ROBIN
These birds are aggressive and males often set up territories in gardens. They sing loudly to keep away other male robins. In winter, both males and females defend feeding territories.

BLUE TITS

These bold, lively birds often visit gardens in winter to feed on nuts, seeds, and leftover food scraps put out by people. They can easily land on nut feeders and often use the nest boxes that people build and put up for them.

Blue tits are agile, acrobatic birds.

Cone-shaped bill typical of a seed eater

WATERFOWL IN PARKS

The artificial lakes in parks make a welcome feeding, resting, and nesting area for geese, ducks, and grebes. Islands in the middle of lakes provide safe nesting places.

NORTHERN CARDINAL

These cardinals are frequent visitors to feeders in the backyards of North America. They often move around in pairs or family groups to feed on seeds that people leave out for them.

SUPERB STARLING

A common visitor to lawns, campsites, and hotels in East Africa, the superb starling is a tame bird, not frightened of people. It feeds mainly on the ground, pecking up seeds, fruit, and insects.

FIELDS AND HEDGEROWS

FARMLAND HAS TAKEN the place of woodlands, grasslands, and wetlands, but some birds have adapted to this habitat. They feed on the crops, and nest in the animal pastures, hedges, orchards, and farm buildings. However, numbers of farmland birds have been reduced by the removal of hedgerows and the use of poisonous pesticides.

GOLDFINCH
Flocks of goldfinches feed on weeds along the edges of fields. They are light enough to perch on thistle heads and eat the seeds.

FOLLOWING THE PLOUGH
Large flocks of birds, such as black-headed gulls, often follow a tractor ploughing a field. The birds feed on the insects and other invertebrates, such as worms, exposed by the plough.

Seagulls following the tractor

PHEASANT
The female common pheasant may nest in hedgerows, making a shallow scrape in the ground in which to lay her eggs. Pheasants wander over farmland, feeding mainly on grains, seeds, berries, and insects.

HOOPOE
In the Mediterranean, the weeds and grasses under the olive groves teem with invertebrates. Hoopoes probe the ground with long curved bills for worms and insects.

DUNNOCK
Sometimes called the hedge sparrow, the dunnock is not related to a sparrow at all – it just looks like one. Dunnocks nest in hedgerows, where they build cup-shaped nests.

The chicks are well camouflaged, like their mother.

The grey head and underparts help to tell the dunnock from a sparrow

FOREST AND WOODLAND

ABOUT THE HABITAT

WITH PLENTY OF FOOD and safe nesting places, forests and woodlands provide a rich habitat for birds, from the treetops right down to the forest floor. A greater variety of birds live in the deciduous and eucalyptus woodlands than in the dark conifer forests, because of the warmer, wetter conditions.

JAY

FOOD AND FEEDING
Woodland birds feed on buds, berries, and seeds from the trees and shrubs. Some eat insects and small animals. Diets may vary with changes in season.

BIRDSONG
Most woodland birds, such as the nightingale, have loud songs and calls to attract mates, and establish breeding territories in the thick undergrowth.

PHEASANT WING

WINGS
Many woodland birds have short, broad, rounded wings to help them rise fast into the air and avoid twigs and branches. Pheasants can fly quickly for short distances.

NIGHTINGALE

NESTS IN HOLES

Holes in trees are safe and warm places for birds such as redstarts to raise a family. In the nesting season, the adults frequently fly in and out with food for the growing young.

MALE
REDSTART

CAMOUFLAGED
WOODCOCK

CAMOUFLAGE

Many woodland and forest birds are well camouflaged to protect them from predators. The dull, mottled colours of this woodcock hide it against the decaying leaf litter of the woodland floor.

Deciduous Woodland

In these temperate woodlands, a great variety of birds can live together because they feed at different levels, sharing out available food. In warm weather, the birds nest, raise their young, and eat as much as possible. In colder weather, the leaves fall off the trees, and some birds migrate to warmer places.

Thick skull

Long, curved claws to cling to tree trunks

Woodpecker
Skull

GOLDEN-FRONTED WOODPECKER
This thrush-sized woodpecker of the Americas hammers into decaying tree trunks to find insect larvae and make nesting holes. It licks up insects with its long, sticky tongue.

Strong, stiff tail feathers for support

LONG-TAILED TITS

Long-tailed tits flit about on the edges of woodlands, pecking insects and spiders off the leaves and bark. Outside the breeding season, the tits huddle in small groups at night to keep warm.

GREEN WOOD HOOPOE

These birds probe tree trunks with their long, curved bills searching for food. They live in noisy family groups in African woodlands.

Long bill is used to find insect grubs or eggs, and spiders.

The bill is broad at the base to catch insects.

SPOTTED FLYCATCHER

Perching on exposed branches, spotted flycatchers dart out to snap up passing insects. In cold weather, they migrate to warmer places, such as Africa, to find food.

Green wood hoopoes have high, cackling calls

WHIP-POOR-WILL

During the day, this well-camouflaged bird sleeps on the woodland floor. At night, it flies near the ground catching insects.

CONIFEROUS FOREST

DARK CONIFEROUS FORESTS – the taiga – stretch across the top of the Northern Hemisphere, from the tundra in the north to the more open deciduous woodlands farther south. The leaves stay on the trees all year round, but winters are bitterly cold and most birds leave for warmer places. In the short summer, they feed on seeds, berries or insects.

CAPERCAILLIE
The capercaillie is able to eat pine needles. This helps it survive through the hard winter. Comb-like fringes on its toes stop it sinking into snow.

SISKIN
The restless and acrobatic siskin often hangs upside-down to pull the seeds out of pine and larch cones. Siskins are social birds and build nests high in conifer trees, where the young cannot easily be reached by enemies.

The siskin feeds on the seeds of pine, larch, alder and birch trees.

RED CROSSBILL

Crossbills use their scissor-
like bills to lever apart the
scales on the cones of pine,
spruce, larch and other
conifers to reach the seeds.
Parent crossbills cough up
partly digested pine seed to
feed to their young.

PINE
CONES

*Scales
opened by a
crossbill*

WAXWING

These birds are named
after the red, wax-like
tips on some of their
flight feathers. Waxwings
eat berries or fruit, but
will also catch insects
when they can. They
migrate south in the
autumn in large numbers.

*Waxwings
live in
large flocks*

*Male and
female birds
are similar
in colour*

JUVENILE BALD EAGLE

Bald eagles live in forests
near water, where they hunt
for fish and waterbirds. They
do not grow the white
feathers on the head and tail
until they are four years old.

EUCALYPTUS WOODLAND

IN THE EVERGREEN eucalyptus woodlands of Australia, there is food and shelter for a variety of unique birds all year. The birds help to pollinate the trees and shrubs, and spread their seeds. In the rainy season, waterbirds gather in marshy areas on the borders of these woodlands.

Strong, hooked beak characteristic of parrot family

MALLEE FOWL
These birds build a huge mound of rotting vegetation covered with sand to keep their eggs warm. The male checks the temperature with his bill.

Two toes in front and two toes behind

RAINBOW LORIKEETS
Noisy flocks of rainbow lorikeets feed high in the trees. They crush the flowers of eucalyptus and other flowering trees to soak up the sticky mixture of nectar and pollen with their fringe-tipped tongues.

Large, broad-based bill to catch and swallow prey

Large head and bill with brown ear patch

LAUGHING KOOKABURRA
Named after its very noisy, chuckling calls, the laughing kookaburra is a giant kingfisher that rarely eats fish. Instead, it pounces on reptiles such as snakes, small mammals, birds, and invertebrates.

OWLS

MOST OWLS SLEEP by day and hunt by night. Their sharp hearing and keen eyesight help them catch prey such as mice and small birds. Many owls roost in trees and have brown feathers for camouflage.

Feathers are fanned out to make owl look frightening

SCOPS OWL

Almost impossible to spot because of its superb camouflage, the scops owl eats large insects. It raises its feathers to defend itself from an

In a complete pellet, animal fur and bones are all stuck together.

Owl mucus binds pellet together

OWL FACTS

- Order *Strigiformes*
- About 174 species
- Mainly nocturnal
- Birds of prey
- Eat birds, insects and small mammals
- Habitat: mainly woodland
- Nest in tree holes, or other birds' nests
- Eggs: white

OWL PELLETS

Once or twice a day, owls cough up pellets containing indigestible bits of their last meal, such as fur or bones. Pulling a pellet apart reveals what an owl has eaten.

BOOBOOK OWL

This small Australian owl gets its name from its double hoot. It feeds mainly on insects.

Large feet with hooked talons

Owls catch and kill prey with their sharp talons.

Barn Owl

A heart-shaped face is the trademark of the barn owl, a bird so different from other owls that it has its own family. The disc of feathers on the face collects sounds like a radar dish. Barn owls make a haunting shrieking sound.

"Ears" are only tufts of feathers

Eurasian Eagle Owl

The largest of all owls, eagle owls are powerful hunters, strong enough to attack hares and mallards. They have very loud hoots: male eagle owls can be heard hooting over 1 km (1/2 mile) away.

BARN OWL
FEATHER

TAWNY
OWL
FEATHER

Owl Feathers

Soft, velvety feathers with fringes on the flight feathers muffle the sound made by the wings in flight.

Thick covering of soft feathers

RAINFORESTS

ABOUT THE HABITAT

TROPICAL RAINFORESTS are the richest bird habitats. They provide a wealth of food and safe nesting places, and a warm, wet climate all year round. Rainforest birds usually have short, broad wings to twist and turn easily when flying through the trees. This unique habitat is under threat from forestry, mining, dams, and farming.

CANOPY

UNDERSTOREY

FOREST FLOOR

BIRDS OF PARADISE

Male birds of paradise have ornate and colourful feathers to attract females. Some tail feathers are very beautiful, like this tail feather from a Count Raggi's bird of paradise.

LAYERS OF LIFE

The birds live at different levels in the trees. In this way, they share the available food and nesting places, so a huge variety of birds can live close together.

SPREADING SEEDS

Fruit-eating birds such as aracaris and parrots help to spread the seeds of rainforest trees. They feed on fruits and pass the seeds in their droppings.

Wide tail helps the aracari to balance on branches

CHESTNUT-EARED
ARACARI

*Long bill with
serrated edge*

*Groups of crested
oropendolas hang
their woven nests
from tree branches.*

NESTING
To keep their nests
out of sight and out of
reach of predators, rainforest birds nest
high in the trees or in dense thickets above
the ground. Some, such as parrots and
hornbills, nest in tree holes.

COLOUR
The bright colours of rainforest
birds like these macaws are
surprisingly hard to see among the
leafy trees. These birds are feeding
on mineral-rich soil.

HABITAT FACTS
• Since 1945, over half
the rainforests have been
destroyed; an area the
size of a soccer pitch is
cut down every second.

• Rainforests contain
over 50 per cent of all
plant and animal species.

• One-fifth of all the
kinds of birds in the
world live in the
Amazon rainforest.

UNDER THE CANOPY

BENEATH THE GREEN ROOF of the forest is the dark, cool understorey of smaller trees, shrubs, and climbing plants, and below this, the leafy forest floor. There is less food and warmth at these lower levels than up in the canopy, so there are fewer birds. Large birds such as trumpeters and cassowaries stalk across the forest floor. In the understorey, hummingbirds and jacamars flit through the branches.

HOATZIN CHICK

HOATZIN
Groups of hoatzins live along riverbanks in the rainforests of South America. They are poor fliers and make short flights through the trees.

Chick has claws on its wings for climbing

DOUBLE-WATTLED CASSOWARY
This huge cassowary melts into the forest if it senses danger. Males make loud, booming calls during courtship. The horny casque on its head is used to push aside forest undergrowth.

SUNBITTERN
This bird is named after the sunset colours on its wings, visible during its courtship display. At other times, it is well camouflaged by the mottled grey and brown colours of its feathers.

Male not
displaying

Courtship
display of male

BLUE BIRDS OF PARADISE
The male blue bird of paradise
performs a dramatic upside-down
display to show off his iridescent
feathers to a female. He also makes a
series of loud, vibrating notes. Females
look after the young on their own.

*These birds live in
the middle or
upper levels of the
rainforest, rarely
coming down to
the ground.*

ASIAN FAIRY BLUEBIRDS
Noisy fairy bluebirds move busily
through the trees searching for
fruit, such as figs. The metallic
blue of the male is not easy to see
in the shade of the trees.

*Fairy bluebirds
often make sharp,
whistling calls.*

IN THE TREETOPS

HIGH UP IN THE RAINFOREST CANOPY it is light
and warm and there is plenty of food, especially
fruits, seeds, and insects. Bird life includes large bird
predators such as eagles which patrol the treetops
looking for prey. Canopy
birds, such as parrots
and toucans, climb well
and have strong feet for
grasping branches.

*Bare, orange-
yellow face
and bill*

HARPY EAGLE
The huge harpy
eagle is one of the most
powerful birds of prey. It
swoops into the canopy to
seize monkeys (like this
capuchin), birds, sloths, and
reptiles. It can fly very fast
through the branches.

LADY ROSS'S TURACO
This African turaco lives in small, noisy
groups, usually high in the canopy.
Although clumsy fliers, turacos are
good at running along tree branches.
They make a great variety of
cackling and croaking calls.

TOCO TOUCAN

This is the largest toucan, with a bill up to 19 cm (7½ in) long. The bill is hollow inside with supporting struts, so it is not as heavy as it looks. The colours help it to recognize other toucans and find a mate.

ORANGE-BELLIED LEAFBIRD

This Asian leafbird helps to pollinate the forest trees as it feeds on nectar. It also spreads the seeds of plants in the mistletoe family by eating the berries.

This leafbird is good at mimicking other birds' songs.

The casque is a thin layer of skin and bone over a honeycomb structure.

GREAT INDIAN HORNBILL

The hornbills of Southeast Asia and Africa look like the toucans of South America because they live and feed in a similar way. They are named after the horny casques on their bills. No-one knows what these bony growths are for.

PARROTS

MOST PARROTS are brightly
coloured and live in
tropical forests. They
tend to fly about in
flocks, making
harsh, screeching
calls. Many
species are threatened by
habitat destruction.
There are three main
groups: the lories, the
cockatoos, and the parrots.

*Narrow, tapering
wings to fly fast
through the trees*

CANARY-
WINGED PARAKEET
This small parrot's
long tail helps it
balance as it flies fast
through the trees. Larger
parrots usually fly more
slowly. One parrot, the
kakapo, cannot fly at all.

CHATTERING LORY
The chattering lory spends most
of its time high in the trees
feeding mainly on pollen
and nectar. Lories have a
brush-like tip to the
tongue which soaks
up their liquid diet.

LESSER SULPHUR-
CRESTED COCKATOO
Cockatoos raise and lower their
head crests when they are
excited, frightened, or
angry. They
also do this
when landing
on a perch.

PARROT FACTS

• Family: Psittacidae

• About 330 species

• Diurnal

• Tropical land birds

• Eat fruits, seeds, nuts,
and other plants; also
some invertebrates

• Habitat: forest,
scrub, grassland, and
mountains

• Nest: usually tree
hole, holes in banks or
among rocks

• Eggs: white

ECLECTUS PARROTS

These parrots are unusual because the bright red female is such a different colour from the green male, whereas male and female parrots usually look alike. Eclectus parrots feed on fruits, nuts, and leaf buds.

SKULL AND BILL

Parrots have broad, large skulls with a fairly big space for the brain – they are intelligent birds. The top bill curves sharply down, fitting neatly over the broad, bottom bill, which curves upwards.

Nutcracker bill to crush seeds and nuts

Many parrots have green feathers to camouflage them in the leaves of the trees.

Two toes point forwards and two backwards to give a powerful grip.

RIVERS, LAKES, AND SWAMPS

ABOUT THE HABITAT

WATERY HABITATS are home to a rich variety of birds, from ducks, coots, and rails to herons and storks. There are plenty of plants, invertebrates, and fish for birds to eat, and safe nesting places in reeds and on riverbanks. Many birds rest and feed on lakes, marshes, and swamps during migration. But drainage schemes, dams, acid rain, and pollution from farms and factories threaten these habitats.

KINGFISHER DIVING

WEBBED FEET FOSSIL

Many waterbirds, such as Canada geese, have webbed feet to push the water aside as they swim. Long legs to wade in deep water, and long toes to walk over soft mud are other common features of waterbirds.

CANADA GOOSE FOOT

HUNTING FOR FISH

To catch fish, birds like this kingfisher dive into the water to seize their prey. Others, such as herons, stand still and catch fish that swim past. Another technique is to scoop up fish from the surface.

CATCHING FISH

Birds need strong bills and feet to hold slippery prey. Mergansers have serrated edges to their bill to help them keep a grip on fish they catch.

HOODED MERGANSER SKULL

NORTHERN SHOVELER

FILTER FEEDING
Birds like the shoveler filter tiny floating plants and animals from water. The shoveler has "combs" on its bill to trap food.

CAMOUFLAGE
The dark, mottled colours of some birds, such as the buff-banded rail, help to camouflage them as they skulk noiselessly through the reed beds of marshes and swamps.

BUFF-BANDED RAIL

NESTING
Hiding a nest away from predators is a relatively easy task in these habitats. Nesting materials such as dried reeds are also easy to find. Some birds even build floating platforms of vegetation for extra security.

HABITAT FACTS

• Lake Baikal in Siberia is the oldest freshwater lake – 25 million years old.

• About six per cent of the Earth's surface is covered by marshes, bogs, and swamps.

• One-fifth of all fresh water on Earth flows through the Amazon River each day.

COOT NESTING IN REEDS

RIVERS AND LAKES

THESE FRESHWATER habitats are important for birds, especially in undisturbed areas free of pollution. Some birds prefer the still waters of ponds and lakes while others, such as dippers, are adapted to move in fast-flowing waters. Around the edge of the water are many places to nest and a variety of food for the young, including water insects.

GREY WAGTAIL
The busy grey wagtail patrols mountain streams, darting out to snap up flying insects in its long bill. It has sharp claws to grip slippery rocks and wet branches.

WESTERN GREBES
The courtship dance of the western grebe is long and unusual. During the dance, a pair stands up tall and races fast across the water with heads tilted forwards.

Long legs to wade through deep water while feeding

Flamingos hold their bills upside down as they filter food

At the last moment, the feet swing forward to grasp the fish.

OSPREY

The osprey is a powerful hunter, plunging feet first into water to snatch fish from near the surface. It sometimes goes right under before pulling up into the air again. Strong claws and spines under the toes help it hold slippery fish.

WHITE-CROWNED FORKTAIL

These Asian birds live by rocky streams, perching on boulders wagging their long tails. They have a loud, high-pitched whistle to communicate above the noise of the water.

All flamingos have some black feathers in their wings.

Lesser flamingos are the smallest of the six species of flamingo.

Crop

LESSER FLAMINGOS

Flamingos live in noisy colonies, sometimes containing thousands of birds. They nest on mounds of mud, and both parents feed the young on a rich "milk" produced in the crop.

SWAMPS AND MARSHES

WET, TREELESS GRASSLANDS, called marshes, and waterlogged forests, called swamps, are often given the name "wetlands". They can be fresh- or saltwater habitats. Fish-eating birds, such as egrets and pelicans, are common, but a lot of birds can feed together by eating different kinds of food at different levels in the water. Wetlands are often refuges for rare birds, as large mammal predators cannot easily hunt there.

SCARLET IBIS
Spectacular flocks of scarlet ibises feed, roost, and nest together in the tropical swamps of South America. Scarlet ibises feel in soft mud or under plants for insects, crabs, shellfish, frogs, and fish. Young scarlet ibises have grey-brown backs for a year while they mature into adults.

Long, thin, down-curved bill to probe for food

Slim body to slide easily through dense vegetation

BLACK CRAKES
These East African birds have long, widely spaced toes to stop them sinking into the mud and help them walk over floating water plants. Their short, thick bills are not long enough to probe in mud, so they peck small invertebrates and seeds off the surface.

BEARDED TIT

Active and acrobatic bearded tits or reedlings fly low over reed beds on their rounded wings. They feed on insects in warm weather, and seeds in cold weather. Both parents build the nest in the reeds and share the care of their young.

WHOOPING CRANES

Among the world's rarest birds, the whooping crane spends the winter on the coastal marshes of Texas, U.S.A. In spring, it migrates to Canada to breed.

Male has black moustache

A bird's "knee" is really its ankle, so it bends backwards, just like a person's ankle.

DUCKS

WEBBED FEET and broad, flat bills are a distinctive feature of ducks. These birds are good swimmers and strong fliers. There are two main types of duck – dabbling ducks, such as the mallard, that feed on the surface, and diving ducks, such as the pochard. Many ducks migrate to avoid cold weather.

FEMALE

MALE

DOWN FEATHERS
Female ducks pluck down feathers from their breasts and use them to line their nests and cover the eggs to keep them warm.

Short legs set well back on body

MANDARIN DUCKS
These ducks live near ponds and lakes surrounded by woods, and nest in tree holes. The male is more colourful than the female, except when he moults his feathers once a year.

CAROLINA OR WOOD DUCK
Found in North America, Carolina ducks are related to Asian Mandarin ducks. The females look after the nest, eggs, and ducklings on their own.

The ducklings swim soon after hatching

DUCK FACTS
• Family: *Anatidae* includes ducks, swans, and geese
• About 152 species
• Diurnal
• Waterfowl
• Eat water plants and small water animals
• Habitat: ponds, lakes, rivers, or the sea
• Nest: platform near water, or in tree holes
• Eggs: white or pale

DIVING DUCKS
These ducks have shorter, rounder bodies than ducks that feed on the surface. Diving ducks, such as this pochard, can stay underwater for 30 seconds or more.

PLUMED WHISTLING DUCK
Whistling ducks live in the tropics and look more like geese than ducks. They feed mainly on the surface.

MALE MALLARD

Webbed feet used like paddles for swimming

Wide, flat bill to sift food out of water

MALLARD DUCK
Mallards feed on the surface of the water or upend to reach plant and animal food a little way below the surface. Mallards are the ancestors of most domestic ducks.

SEAS, CLIFFS, AND SHORES

ABOUT THE HABITAT

SOME SPECIALLY adapted birds spend most of their lives gliding over the open oceans. But they nest on shores and in the safety of cliff ledges, usually in large colonies. The rich feeding grounds of estuaries attract huge numbers of waders and wildfowl, especially on migration.

FLIGHT

Seabirds such as the fulmar have long, narrow wings to glide fast over the waves for long distances. However, they are not very good at walking, and are clumsy and ungainly on land.

FULMAR IN FLIGHT

Fulmars have tube-shaped nostrils above the bill. Albatrosses and petrels are also tube-nosed birds.

Fulmars have a stiff-winged flight, hardly bending their wings at all.

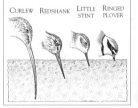

CURLEW	REDSHANK	LITTLE STINT	RINGED PLOVER

FEEDING

Finding food out at sea is not always easy, and seabirds spend most of their time looking for the next meal. Terns dive to take fish at or near the surface. Other seabirds, such as puffins, swim deeper underwater.

PUFFIN WITH CATCH

SHARING FEEDING PLACES

Some waders feed close together because their bills are different lengths to feed at different levels in the mud or sand. The curlew's long bill reaches worms in deep burrows, while the ringed plover picks insects off the surface.

HERRING
GULL EGGS

Most seabird eggs are more pointed at one end than the other.

CAMOUFLAGED EGGS
Birds such as gulls or terns have camouflaged eggs, as they nest in the open on beaches or dunes. The spots and other markings help the eggs to blend into the background so predators find it hard to see them.

GANNET
ON NEST

NESTING
Many seabirds nest in tightly packed colonies of thousands or even millions of birds. The vast numbers stimulate them to breed at the same time. Gannets nest close together in noisy, smelly colonies.

HABITAT FACTS

• Oceans cover about 70 per cent of the Earth's surface.

• The sea cools more slowly than the land, keeping coastal areas warmer in winter.

• The tidal range in open oceans is only about 50 cm (20 in).

• In 1 sq m (10 sq ft) of estuary there may be over 1,000 worms.

ESTUARIES AND SHORES

APART FROM CLIFFS, other areas
along the shoreline, such as dunes
and beaches, provide nesting areas
for seabirds. And where rivers
meet the sea, the shallow, muddy
waters of estuaries teem with a
wealth of food such as
fish, worms, and shellfish.
Estuaries are particularly
important in cold
weather, when inland
feeding areas
are frozen.

PURPLE SANDPIPER
Stocky purple sandpipers
migrate south in colder
weather to feed on rocky
shores. They search the
shoreline for food, finding
their prey by sight rather
than by touch.

BLACK-NECKED STILT
This stilt has extremely
long legs which allow it
to feed in deeper water
than other waders. It
uses its long bill to take
small creatures from
water and mud.

*On dry ground,
the stilt bends its
legs awkwardly
to feed.*

*In flight, the stilt's legs
stick out 18 cm (7 in)
beyond the tail to
counterbalance the
head and neck.*

SLEEPING
On an estuary, waders such
as this dunlin feed when they
can, and sleep when the tide
comes in and covers their
feeding grounds. They flock
to the safety of high-tide
roosts, such as small islands.

INCA TERN
This South American tern often gathers in flocks of many thousands, and roosts on sandy beaches. Inca terns are graceful fliers, hovering over the sea, and dipping down to snatch food from the surface.

Inca terns may follow whales and seals to seize scraps of food.

GREAT BLACK-BACKED GULL
These huge gulls are fierce predators of seabird colonies on the coast. They have long, powerful wings for gliding.

RINGED PLOVER
As soon as the ringed plover stops moving, its colours make it hard to see among the pebbles on the beach. Females may pretend to be injured to draw predators away from eggs and young.

SEA AND CLIFFS

OVER THE OPEN OCEAN, seabirds search for food, also landing on the surface to rest and preen. Seabirds have waterproofed feathers, webbed feet for swimming, and sharp bills to catch slippery prey. Many nest on cliffs where eggs and young are safe from predators.

NESTING SPACE
To share the nesting sites on a cliff, the birds nest at different levels. Gannets, and kittiwakes nest near the top, and razorbills in the middle. Shags and cormorants nest lower down.

After fishing, the cormorant holds its wings open to dry.

GANNET SKULL
To catch fish, gannets plunge into the sea like torpedos from heights of up to 30 m (100 ft). They have a strong skull to withstand the impact when they hit the water with such a great force.

COMMON CORMORANT
The feathers of the common or great cormorant trap very little air, so the bird sinks in water more easily than other seabirds and can feed on bottom-living creatures.

A frigatebird robs a tropicbird of its fishy meal.

PIRACY AT SEA

Frigatebirds steal much of their food from other birds such as pelicans and gulls. They are speedy fliers and can swoop, dart, soar, and hover better than most other seabirds.

Nests of grass, seaweeds and mud sit snugly on narrow ledges.

KITTIWAKES

These small gulls nest close together in colonies consisting of hundreds of birds. They are named after their call. Unlike other gulls they are rarely found on land.

DESERTS, SCRUB, AND GRASSLANDS

ABOUT THE HABITAT

IN THESE MAINLY HOT, dry habitats, birds may have to travel long distances to find food and water, or migrate to avoid dry seasons. Seeds and insects are the main sources of food, but some larger birds also feed on reptiles, small mammals, and dead animals. In the heat of the day, most birds are less active and rest in the shade.

Bee-eaters feed mainly on honeybees.

INSECT EATERS

Birds such as bee-eaters and warblers feed on the insects which are most abundant during a rainy season. In the dry season, insect eaters often have to migrate to find enough to eat.

White-throated bee-eaters fly to wetter grasslands in the dry season.

ROADRUNNER

VARIED DIET

Food is often hard to find, so birds survive by eating any food they come across. Reptiles are a common source of food. This roadrunner has caught a lizard.

WHITE-THROATED BEE-EATER

These birds are threatened by the caged bird trade.

SEED EATERS

Grass seeds are a vital source of food for many birds, such as these Australian Gouldian finches. When the grasses die back in the dry season, the finches migrate towards wetter areas on the coast.

GOULDIAN
FINCHES

RUBBISH CLEARANCE

The carcasses of large grazing animals and human rubbish tips provide food for birds such as marabou storks and vultures.

BURROWING
OWLS

UNDERGROUND SHELTERS

To keep out of the heat of the Sun, burrowing owls rest and nest safe from enemies inside burrows dug by small mammals like prairie dogs.

MARABOU
STORK

HABITAT FACTS

• More than a quarter of all the land on Earth is covered in grass.

• Deserts have less than 25 mm (10 in) rainfall each year.

• In the deserts of Death Valley, U.S.A., temperatures can reach as high as 55°C (131°F).

• The African ostrich is the heaviest, tallest and fastest-running bird in the world.

DESERTS

BIRDS THAT LIVE in deserts have to get most of their water either from their food or by flying long distances. By day, they may rest in the shade of rocks, or inside cacti or underground burrows. Some come out to feed at night, when it is cooler. Many birds of prey survive in deserts on a diet of reptiles and small mammals.

SANDGROUSE
These birds are strong fliers and travel many kilometres to find water. The male birds carry water back to their chicks in their belly feathers.

Hooked beak typical of bird of prey

ELF OWL
The sparrow-sized elf owl nests in holes dug out by woodpeckers inside giant saguaro cacti. The spines of the cactus protect the eggs and young from predators. Elf owls hunt for insects in the cool of the night.

It is much cooler inside the cactus.

HARRIS' HAWK
A fearless hunter of birds, lizards, and small mammals, Harris's hawk sometimes feeds on carcasses, alongside vultures and caracaras. It is often found near roadsides in the desert regions of the Americas.

The female does not have orange cheek patches and her bill is a duller red.

The male has zebra-like stripes on the chest.

ZEBRA FINCHES
These lively little birds are common in the Australian outback. They nest after the rains when there are plenty of seeds and insects to feed to their young. They live in flocks of up to 100 birds, and several may nest together.

SCRUB AND BUSH

THE BIRDS OF these warm, dry, dusty habitats may roam widely in search of food, or follow the rains. The thorny bushes and shrubs often form dense thickets and these make safe nesting places. The berries that grow on the bushes and shrubs can be a useful source of food in colder weather.

COCKATIELS
These small cockatoos wander over the Australian bush country looking for fruits and grass seeds. They usually nest after rainfall at any time of year.

Males have brighter markings on the face than the females.

BLUE-CAPPED CORDON-BLEU
Small groups of cordon-bleus search the ground for grass seeds and insects in the thorn scrub of East Africa. They feed their young mainly on a protein-rich diet of insects.

Short, stubby bill to crush seeds

INDIAN GREY FRANCOLIN

These birds are common in southern
Asia because they are able to survive
in dry conditions. They usually live in
small family groups, and feed
on weed seeds and grain
crops. In warm weather,
they also eat
insects.

*Francolins try to
escape danger by
running.*

SCRUBLAND

The scrubland habitats of small trees and
thorny shrubs are halfway between
grassland and woodland. They include
the Mediterranean scrublands, the
Californian chaparral, and parts of the
Australian bush or outback.

EMU

Small flocks of flightless
emus roam widely through the
Australian bush in search of
seeds, berries, and insects.
The male looks after
the chicks for
up to 18 months.

WHITE HELMET SHRIKE

Tame and active white helmet
shrikes live in small flocks of
two to 20 birds. They hop
through the African bush
snapping up insects and spiders
with their strong, hooked bills.

GRASSLANDS

A VARIETY OF seed- and insect-eating birds live in grasslands, especially those birds that can adapt to living near people. Some birds follow herds of grazing animals to snap up the insects disturbed by their feet. Other birds feed on the animals when they die. Long legs enable birds such as ostriches and rheas to see over tall grasses and watch for danger.

Oxpeckers and giraffe

OXPECKERS

These birds pick ticks and insects off the fur of large African mammals such as giraffes and zebra. They cling to the mammal's fur with their sharp claws.

In breeding plumage, male is bright chestnut, with black head and throat

This weaver is a shy bird, with a fast, dashing flight.

CHESTNUT WEAVER

These weavers nest in dense colonies in the African grasslands. Out of the breeding season, both male and female are dull brown.

OSTRICH

Able to survive in very dry conditions, ostriches stride over the African savannah grasslands on their long legs, searching for leaves, seeds, and insects. They are threatened by hunting and habitat destruction.

Bare head
and neck

HOODED VULTURE
The bare head
and neck of the
hooded vulture allow it to
reach right inside an animal
carcass to feed without getting
its feathers dirty. Vultures fly
high, using their sharp eyesight
to spot carrion.

Sometimes called
the ovenbird because
the nest looks like
an old-fashioned
baker's oven

Strong talons
cling onto branch

RUFOUS HORNERO
There are few trees on the South
American pampas grasslands, so the
rufous hornero builds a huge mud nest to
protect its eggs and young. The nest is
made of mud and straw baked by the Sun.

MOUNTAINS AND MOORLAND

ABOUT THE HABITAT

MOORLANDS TEND TO BE wet, boggy places while mountains can be very cold and windy. Only a few hardy birds live on mountains and moorland because of the harsh climate and lack of food, especially in the cold seasons. However, these habitats are important breeding areas for birds.

This shy, secretive bird rarely emerges from the bamboo thickets and dense forest where it lives.

SEASONAL MIGRATION
Hardy pheasants such as this Lady Amherst's pheasant live in the mountain forests of Asia. They move up and down the mountains with the seasons. Many pheasants are threatened by hunting.

Feathered feet to insulate against the cold

Colourful feathers and neck ruff

LADY AMHERST'S PHEASANT

CAMOUFLAGE
In autumn, the ptarmigan grows new white feathers for camouflage. These tough birds bury themselves in snow to keep out cold, biting winds. In summer, their plumage is mottled grey-brown.

NESTING
CURLEW

MOUNTAIN FORESTS

The warmer forests on the
lower slopes of mountains
provide many birds with
plenty of food and
nesting places. In
colder weather,
birds may move
down to these
forests from
the upper
slopes.

RUFOUS-
BELLIED
NILTAVA

*These Asian
flycatchers live in
mountain forest
above 1,000 m
(3,000 ft).*

NESTING PLACES

Waders such as this curlew nest
on windswept moorland in
summer. They hide their nests
among grasses and bushes.
Their young feed on insects,
worms, frogs, and snails. In
winter, they move to the coast.

GROUSE
EGG

MOORLAND EGGS

Heavy blotches of colour help
to camouflage the eggs of
moorland nesters such as
grouse and waders
among the heather
and bracken. The
eggs are laid in a
shallow scrape
on the ground.

CURLEW
EGG

*Male has long
tail for display*

HABITAT FACTS

• The Appalachians
were formed over 250
million years ago; the
Himalayas formed only
40 million years ago.

• The world's longest
mountain chain is the
Andes at 7,250 km
(4,500 miles) long.

• Some moorland is
created by a change to a
wetter climate; others
by people clearing trees
for farmland.

MOUNTAINS

IN COLD WEATHER, food is scarce on mountains, but these areas are undisturbed breeding areas for birds. Birds' feathers keep them warm when it is freezing cold, and efficient lungs enable them to get enough oxygen from the thin air. Many mountain birds are powerful fliers.

RAVEN
These large members of the crow family are mainly scavengers. They patrol the mountain slopes, searching for food with their sharp eyes.

WALLCREEPER
This nimble bird clings on to rock faces with its sharp claws, probing for insects with its slender bill. In cold weather, it moves to lower slopes where there are more insects for it to eat.

SWORD-BILLED HUMMINGBIRD
This hummingbird lives high in the Andes. It has a very long bill, which it uses to sip nectar from flowers.

SNOW, ICE, AND ROCK

GRASSY MEADOWS

CONIFEROUS FOREST

TEMPERATE FOREST

HABITAT ZONES
Mountains have a variety of habitats. There are warm, deciduous forests on the lower slopes, cooler coniferous forests higher up, and, just below the snow-covered peaks, grasslands and scrub.

The lammergeier is also called the bearded vulture.

Lammergeiers fly to great heights and drop bones on to rocks to break them apart.

LAMMERGEIER
Soaring over the mountain slopes on rising warm air currents, the lammergeier searches the steep slopes for the carcasses of animals killed by the harsh climate. It drops the bones onto rocks to smash them open, then scoops out the marrow with its long tongue.

ANDEAN CONDOR
The world's heaviest bird of prey, the Andean condor, has very keen eyesight and long, broad wings. It soars over the Andes looking for dead, sick, or wounded animals to feed on. There is a ready supply of food because of the difficult living conditions.

MOORLAND

THIS WATERLOGGED habitat of grasses and low-growing shrubs is found in cool, upland areas with lots of rain. It is an important breeding ground for waders and grouse. Predators such as hen harriers and golden eagles find many small birds and mammals to eat here, and there are plenty of insects breeding in the peaty bogs.

Upper parts have golden colour all year round.

Golden plovers feed on insects, worms, and seeds.

GOLDEN PLOVER
In late spring, golden plovers migrate to moorland to breed. They lay their well-camouflaged eggs in a shallow scrape in the ground.

STONECHAT
The restless stonechat perches on bushes and posts to watch for insects, worms, and spiders. It builds a nest of moss, grass, and hair, well hidden in bushes or thick grass.

PEREGRINE FALCON
These falcons stoop at an incredible speed to kill prey such as golden plover or pigeons with their talons. They pluck the feathers from prey before eating the flesh.

RED GROUSE
This bird is a distinctive sub-species of the willow grouse or willow ptarmigan. Many moorlands are carefully managed to keep a lot of these birds for shooting in the autumn grouse season.

Birds such as red grouse shelter, hide, and nest in heather.

Some stonechats migrate to warmer places in cold weather.

EAGLES

WITH THEIR SHARP EYES, huge wings, and strong legs and feet, eagles are the most powerful of the birds of prey. Females are usually larger than males. Many species of eagle are threatened by people hunting them, poisoning them, and destroying their habitat.

Light-coloured crown and neck feathers

Strong talons to grip and crush prey

COURTSHIP
During courtship, many eagles show off their amazing flying skills. A pair of bald eagles will tumble and spin through the sky, while trying to touch or grip one another's talons.

Courtship display of bald eagles

IMPERIAL EAGLE
Feathered legs are a characteristic of the imperial eagle, which belongs to a group called the booted eagles. It is widespread in parts of Asia, but rare in Europe.

GOLDEN EAGLE
These eagles are strong fliers, soaring high on outstretched wings to search for prey. They are named after the golden feathers on the top of the head and the back of the neck.

Primary flight feathers for power and steering

BATELEUR EAGLE

This eagle's name comes from the French word for "juggler" because of its aerial courtship display. It has long wings and a short tail. When it is excited or angry, its crest is raised.

Raised crest

A bald eagle's eyrie

EYRIE

Eagle nests are called eyries and bald eagles have made some of the biggest eyries in the world. They use the same nest year after year, adding more and more twigs and sticks each time they nest.

EAGLE FACTS

• Family: *Accipitridae* – includes snake eagles and booted eagles

• About 53 species

• Diurnal

• Birds of prey

• Eat a variety of animals, alive and dead

• Habitat: wide range

• Nest: mass of sticks in tree or on cliff ledge

• Eggs: white or marked with brown

POLAR
AND TUNDRA
REGIONS

ABOUT THE HABITAT

THE FROZEN POLAR REGIONS are the coldest and windiest places on Earth. Few birds can survive there all year round. Most migrate there to breed in the short summer months, when the Sun shines 24 hours a day and there is plenty of food. These unique habitats are threatened by mining, tourism, and pollution.

TUNDRA LANDSCAPES
Around the edge of the Arctic Ocean lie the flat tundra lands, which have a frozen layer called permafrost under the ground. In summer, the soil above the permafrost thaws out, and lakes and marshes form on the surface.

Tundra means "barren land" in Finnish

Ice floating on water

Shoreline

Tundra with permafrost under the ground

Marshy tundra landscape in summer

MIGRATION
In summer, millions of ducks, swans, and geese, such as the barnacle goose, migrate to the tundra lands to feed and nest there. They eat new vegetation sprouting from the warm, moist ground.

LITTLE AUK

ADAPTATIONS
The Arctic auks look like the Antarctic penguins. They have flipper-like wings for swimming, but unlike penguins, they can fly.

KEEPING WARM

Birds such as the eider duck cover their eggs with soft down which the female plucks from her own breast. This helps to keep the eggs warm until they are read to hatch.

PENGUIN FLIPPER

SWIMMING

Many birds of these habitats are good swimmers. Penguins have stiff, densely packed scale-like feathers on their wings to reduce the drag of the water against them when swimming.

EIDER DUCK NEST

LAPLAND BUNTING

FACTS

• Antarctica has 90 per cent of all the ice on Earth and 70 per cent of all the water.

• Permafrost under the tundra can be up to 1,400 m (3,840 ft) thick.

• The Arctic is an ice-covered ocean surrounded by land – Antarctica is frozen land surrounded by ocean.

FOOD

The tundra summer is brief, but thousands of insects swarm over marshy pools. So birds like the Lapland bunting have plenty of food to collect for their young.

ARCTIC AND TUNDRA

AROUND THE NORTH POLE is a huge ice-covered ocean surrounded by tundra landscape. This region is called the Arctic. In summer months, gulls, auks, and terns feed on the fish at sea, and nest on the coast. The insects and seeds on the tundra are food for waders, ducks, geese, and small songbirds. Before winter, the birds fly south to warmer regions.

Male giving his mate a fishy gift during courtship

ARCTIC TERNS
After courtship, terns raise their young in the Arctic summer, then fly all the way to Antarctica for the summer there. They do an incredible round trip of 35,000 km (22,000 miles).

SNOWY OWL FOOT

SNOWY OWL
The plumage of the snowy owl camouflages it against the Arctic landscape, as it glides over the ground looking for prey. Feathers on its legs and feet help it to keep warm.

COMMON REDPOLL
This little bird can survive low temperatures. It eats a lot of seeds, and some small insects and their larvae in summer. Some redpolls nest in dwarf birches near the ground in tundra habitats.

Redpolls are named after their red forehead, or "poll".

EMPEROR GOOSE
This handsome, grey goose breeds along marshy shores in Alaska. Some birds may migrate south to northern California in winter.

Adults have orange legs.

In winter, the male snow bunting turns browner and looks more like the female.

SNOW BUNTING
Hardy snow buntings breed in the Arctic – farther north than any other perching bird. They usually hide their nest from predators in crannies in the rocks.

Snow buntings may burrow in the snow to escape intense cold.

ANTARCTICA

THIS VAST AREA of frozen land surrounded by ocean has little rain or snow, so the birds have little fresh water to drink, apart from melted snow. The only two land birds are sheathbills. All the others are seabirds, including albatrosses, petrels, and penguins, millions of which nest around Antarctic coasts in summer. The seabirds have dense feathers or layers of fat to keep warm, and are strong swimmers or fliers.

BROWN SKUA
With their hooked bills and strong claws, skuas are fierce predators of penguin eggs and chicks. In summer, they regularly patrol penguin colonies in Antarctica.

ADELIE PENGUINS
Adelies are one of the two species of penguin that nest on the rocky coasts of Antarctica itself. In spring, they march inland from the sea to nest on the ground in huge rookeries.

BLACK-BROWED ALBATROSSES
Albatrosses mate for life and reinforce the pair bond each year when they return to the nest. This pair is bill-touching and preening each other.

The only bird found in Antarctica that does not have webbed feet

SNOWY SHEATHBILL
A relative of pigeons, this bird scavenges around seal and penguin colonies as well as searching the shoreline for fish, invertebrates, and shellfish. Sheathbills live in small flocks, except in the breeding season.

IMPERIAL SHAGS
These impressive birds nest in large colonies on coastal ledges or among rocks. They have strong, hooked bills to grasp slippery fish. In the breeding season, they grow wispy crests.

BLACK-BROWED ALBATROSSES

Nest is a big heap of mud and grass about 60 cm (24 in) high

PENGUINS

WITH THEIR SMOOTH, streamlined shape, and stiff, strong wings, penguins are expert swimmers. They dive to catch fish and squid with their spiky tongues. Dense, oily feathers, and thick fat under the skin keep them warm in the cold southern oceans. Penguins only come out of the water to moult and breed, some in colonies of thousands of millions.

EMPEROR PENGUINS
These are the biggest penguins. They never come on land, but breed on the ice that floats around Antarctica in winter. Males incubate the single egg for about nine weeks.

KING PENGUINS
The striking golden-orange ear patches of these birds are used for display during courtship. The markings also help them to recognize other king penguins. These large penguins can dive down as deep as 250 m (850 ft).

Powerful, narrow wings for swimming

Stiff tail feathers used to support body on land

Male king penguin incubates egg against bare patch of warm skin

Porpoising Adelie penguins

In water, penguins look dark from above and pale from below – this helps to camouflage them

SWIMMING AND DIVING

In order to breathe while swimming fast, penguins leap in and out of the water. This technique is called porpoising. They can travel through water in this way at over 30 km/h (20 mph), using their stiff wings to push themselves along.

MACARONI PENGUIN

During their courtship displays, these birds shake their bright yellow head crests. The crests also help them to recognize other macaronis.

Spread flippers cool bird down

Feet well back on body to act as rudder

CHINSTRAP PENGUIN

These penguins are named because of the black line under their chin. They are noisy and quarrelsome birds.

PENGUIN FACTS
- Family: *Spheniscidae*
- About 18 species
- Diurnal and nocturnal
- Flightless seabirds
- Eat fish, squid, and small sea creatures
- Habitat: southern oceans, cool temperate islands, tropical shores
- Nest: stones, grass, mud, caves, or burrows
- Eggs: whitish

REFERENCE SECTION

BIRD CLASSIFICATION

THE PROCESS OF CLASSIFICATION puts living things,
such as birds, into groups based on features that
they have in common. It is a way of organizing our
knowledge about birds, and may or may not
consider their evolutionary history. Birds are divided
into a series of increasingly narrow categories,
starting with the largest
group, the kingdom.

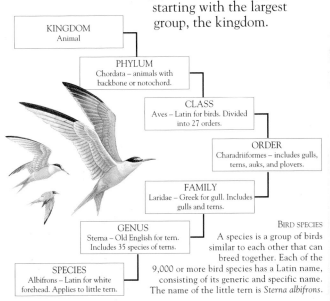

KINGDOM
Animal

PHYLUM
Chordata – animals with
backbone or notochord.

CLASS
Aves – Latin for birds. Divided
into 27 orders.

ORDER
Charadriiformes – includes gulls,
terns, auks, and plovers.

FAMILY
Laridae – Greek for gull. Includes
gulls and terns.

GENUS
Sterna – Old English for tern.
Includes 35 species of terns.

SPECIES
Albifrons – Latin for white
forehead. Applies to little tern.

BIRD SPECIES
A species is a group of birds
similar to each other that can
breed together. Each of the
9,000 or more bird species has a Latin name,
consisting of its generic and specific name.
The name of the little tern is *Sterna albifrons*.

FAMILY	SPECIES	CHARACTERISTICS
STRUTHIONIFORMES *(1 species in family)*	Ostrich	Large flightless African bird, long neck and legs, two toes
RHEIFORMES *(2 species in family)*	Rheas	Large, flightless South American birds, three toes
CASUARIIFORMES *(4 species in family)*	Cassowaries and emu	Large, flightless Australasian birds, three toes
APTERYGIFORMES *(3 species in family)*	Kiwis	Medium-sized, flightless New Zealand birds, nocturnal, good sense of smell
TINAMIFORMES *(46 species in family)*	Tinamous	Gamebird-like species from Central and South America, poor fliers, ground-dwelling
SPHENISCIFORMES *(18 species in family)*	Penguins	Flightless, swimming seabirds with flipper-like wings, webbed feet, dense plumage, usually blue-black above, white below
GAVIIFORMES *(5 species in family)*	Divers	Large swimming and diving birds, with webbed feet, pointed bill and long, thin neck
PODICIPEDIFORMES *(21 species in family)*	Grebes	Small- to medium-sized swimming and diving birds, with lobed feet, pointed bill and long, thin neck
PROCELLARIIFORMES *(110 species in family)*	Albatrosses, fulmars, petrels, shearwaters, storm-petrels, diving-petrels	Seabirds with tube-like nostrils, good sense of smell, long wings. Come to land only to breed, slow development

FAMILY	SPECIES	CHARACTERISTICS
PELECANIFORMES *(62 species in family)*	Tropicbirds, pelicans, gannets and boobies, cormorants and shags, darters and anhingas, frigatebirds	Fish-eating, mostly marine birds with three webs linking four toes. Some have expandable throat pouch
CICONIIFORMES *(117 species in family)*	Herons and bitterns, storks, ibises and spoonbills, hammerkop, whale-headed stork, flamingos	Large wading birds with long legs and long bill, mainly eat fish and amphibians, also large insects. Flamingos filter feeders
ANSERIFORMES *(150 species in family)*	Screamers, ducks, geese, swans	Semi-aquatic wildfowl with well-developed down, a feathered preen gland, and round, open nostrils
FALCONIFORMES *(290 species in family)*	Vultures, osprey, hawks and eagles, secretary bird, falcons and caracaras	Small to large diurnal birds of prey; some are scavengers (vultures), others hunters (falcons)
GALLIFORMES *(274 species in family)*	Megapodes, curassows and guans, pheasants and grouse, turkeys, guineafowl	Ground-dwelling gamebirds. Young leave nest soon after hatching
GRUIFORMES *(190 species in family)*	Mesites, button quails, plains-wanderer, cranes, limpkin, rails, coots, trumpeters, finfoots, kagu, sunbittern, seriemas, bustards	Ground dwelling, many live in wet habitats, most nest on ground or make floating nests
CHARADRIIFORMES *(337 species in family)*	Waders, gulls, terns, skuas, skimmers, auks	Diverse group of aquatic, often marine birds, may be web-footed, variety of bills
COLUMBIFORMES *(300 species in family)*	Pigeons, doves, sandgrouse	Land birds with long, pointed wings, short legs, small feet, small head and bill
PSITTACIFORMES *(342 species in family)*	Parrots, lories, cockatoos	Colourful tropical land birds with powerful hooked bill, four toes (two front and two back). Often long-lived, some good mimics

FAMILY	SPECIES	CHARACTERISTICS
CUCULIFORMES (159 species in family)	Turacos, cuckoos, hoatzin	Land birds with four toes (two front and two back), bill not hooked. Some cuckoos parasitic. Hoatzin unique
STRIGIFORMES (174 species in family)	Barn owls, owls	Mostly nocturnal or crepuscular birds of prey with good hearing, large, immovable eyes, facial disc, silent flight, strong talons
CAPRIMULGIFORMES (109 species in family)	Oilbird, frogmouths, potoos, owlet-nightjars, nightjars	Mainly nocturnal or crepuscular birds with camouflaged colours and wide bill to scoop up insects. Oilbird feeds on fruit
APODIFORMES (429 species in family)	Swifts, tree swifts, hummingbirds	Agile fliers with very short upper arm and small feet. Hummingbirds tiny nectar-feeders with fast wingbeats
COLIIFORMES (6 species in family)	Mousebirds	Small, African birds with long, pointed, graduated tails, short wings and legs, and stout, hooked bill
TROGONIFORMES (39 species in family)	Trogons	Mainly fruit-eating, tropical forest birds, with small, weak feet and legs, long squarish tail, brightly coloured plumage
CORACIIFORMES (204 species in family)	Kingfishers, todies, motmots, bee-eaters, rollers, ground rollers, cuckoo roller, hoopoe, wood-hoopoe, hornbills	Carnivorous land birds with large bills. Usually brightly coloured with two front toes joined for all or part of the length
PICIFORMES (381 species in family)	Jacamars, puffbirds, barbets, honeyguides, woodpeckers	Four toes (two forward and two back), many forest dwellers, variety of bill shapes and sizes
PASSERIFORMES (5,414 species in family)	Includes pittas, starlings, swallows, leafbirds, birds of paradise, thrushes, warblers, chickadees, sunbirds, finches	Largest order with 75 families and 60 per cent of all birds. Perching land birds with four toes (three forward, one back)

BIRDWATCHING

TO REALLY UNDERSTAND birds, you need to watch them yourself. Choose warm, waterproof clothes that are well camouflaged, and take a notebook. A pair of binoculars is vital; a camera or tape recorder may also be useful.

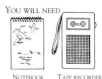

YOU WILL NEED

NOTEBOOK   TAPE RECORDER

BINOCULARS   CAMERA
8 X 30 MM   35 MM SLR

HIDES
Birds are (with good reason) suspicious of people. To get close to them, you will need to hide behind bushes or fences, and stalk quietly and slowly. The best cover is a hide, especially when the birds are nesting. A car can make a good hide.

Vertical slit in wall for watching birds

Old sheet or canvas painted green or brown

Framework of sticks tied with string or wire

FLIGHT SHAPES

You may only catch a glimpse of many birds, especially birds of prey, flying high overhead. Learning to recognize flight shapes like the ones below will help you to identify birds even when you cannot see them clearly.

Eagle – wide wings and tail, finger-like wingtips

Heron – bowed wings, head tucked back, feet trailing

Swallow – long, forked tail, pointed wings

Gull – long, narrow wings

Goose – wide wings with pointed tips, neck stretched out

Crow – broad, pointed wings with slotted tips, long tail

KEEPING A NOTEBOOK

Sketching the birds you don't know will help you identify them later, and you don't have to be able to draw well. First draw a rough outline of the bird; then note its colour, shape, flight pattern, and behaviour. You can also jot down where and when you saw the bird, and what the weather was like.

BIRDWATCHING CODE

• Always avoid disturbing birds, particularly if they have eggs or young.

• Never touch, handle, or collect eggs and nests.

• If you see a baby bird on its own, leave it alone; one of its parents is probably nearby.

TRACKS AND SIGNS

YOU WILL NEED

TWEEZERS

MAGNIFYING GLASS

RULER SAMPLE BAG

STUDYING TRACKS and signs that birds leave behind will tell you a lot about their behaviour and diet. Food remains, feathers, eggshells, and droppings provide clues, as do footprints. Pellets, the undigested remains of a bird's meals, are also useful signs. Birds of prey produce pellets, but so do other birds such as gulls and crows.

FEATHERS
You may find feathers that have been moulted, or discarded after a bird has been eaten.

WADER CROW SONGBIRD

PELLETS
Good places to look for bird pellets include nest sites, feeding sites, and roosting places.

RECORDING TRACKS
A plaster cast of a bird track gives an accurate record which you can build up into a permanent collection. Plaster of Paris is available at most chemist shops.

JUG OF WATER BOWL AND SPOON PLASTER OF PARIS

STRIP OF CARD PAPER CLIPS

Join the ends together with a paper clip.

1 Look for a good, clear bird track left in wet mud or damp ground. Bend a strip of card around it and join the ends with a paper clip. Push the card a little way into the ground.

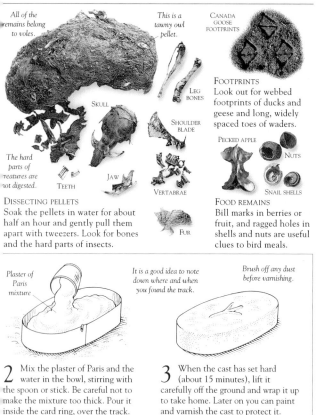

All of the remains belong to voles.

This is a tawny owl pellet.

CANADA GOOSE FOOTPRINTS

SKULL

LEG BONES

SHOULDER BLADE

The hard parts of creatures are not digested.

TEETH

JAW

VERTEBRAE

FUR

PECKED APPLE

NUTS

SNAIL SHELLS

FOOTPRINTS

Look out for webbed footprints of ducks and geese and long, widely spaced toes of waders.

DISSECTING PELLETS

Soak the pellets in water for about half an hour and gently pull them apart with tweezers. Look for bones and the hard parts of insects.

FOOD REMAINS

Bill marks in berries or fruit, and ragged holes in shells and nuts are useful clues to bird meals.

Plaster of Paris mixture

It is a good idea to note down where and when you found the track.

Brush off any dust before varnishing.

2 Mix the plaster of Paris and the water in the bowl, stirring with the spoon or stick. Be careful not to make the mixture too thick. Pour it inside the card ring, over the track.

3 When the cast has set hard (about 15 minutes), lift it carefully off the ground and wrap it up to take home. Later on you can paint and varnish the cast to protect it.

FEEDING THE BIRDS

IN COLD WEATHER, you can help birds survive by putting out food. In warm weather, there is plenty of natural food about so there is less need to lend a hand. Remember to put out water as well as food.

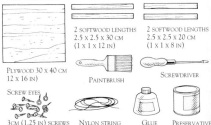

Gaps for rainwater to drain off

Try to identify the birds that visit the table regularly

BIRD TABLE

Encourage birds to visit you by making a bird table. Hang the table from a branch or windowsill, or fix it to the end of a stake in the ground. Position the table about 1.2-.1.5 m (4-5 ft) off the ground and no more than 3.5-5 m (12-16 ft) away from cover. Clean·the table every so often.

YOU WILL NEED

PLYWOOD 30 x 40 CM
12 x 16 IN)

2 SOFTWOOD LENGTHS
2.5 x 2.5 x 30 CM
(1 x 1 x 12 IN)

2 SOFTWOOD LENGTHS
2.5 x 2.5 x 20 CM
(1 x 1 x 8 IN)

PAINTBRUSH

SCREWDRIVER

SCREW EYES

3CM (1.25 IN) SCREWS   NYLON STRING   GLUE   PRESERVATIVE

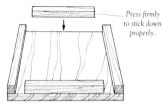

Press firmly to stick down properly.

1 Glue the four thin strips of wood or dowel to the edges of the plywood, as shown. There should be a gap in each corner.

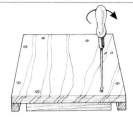

2 Turn the table over and screw the sides down to hold them firmly in position. Put in two screws on every side as shown.

Press hard on the paint brush

3 Paint the wood with a wood preservative that is not harmful to wildlife. Leave it to dry completely before the next step.

4 Put two screw-eyes at the base of each short side and thread string or nylon thread through the holes. Your bird table is ready to hang.

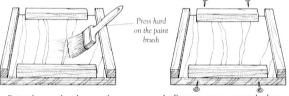

FOOD FOR THE TABLE

A wide range of food will attract a variety of birds. For a bird pudding, mix food such as seeds or nuts with the same amount of melted suet or fat.

| SEED PUDDING | NUT PUDDING | MEALWORMS | COCONUT | PEANUTS | NUT BASKET |

ENDANGERED BIRDS

OVER TEN PER CENT of the world's birds are endangered and about half of these live on islands. The parrot family is the most at risk, with over 70 species threatened. In the past, people have hunted some birds, such as the passenger pigeon and the dodo, to extinction. Today, hunting is still a threat to birds, but other human activities, especially habitat destruction, are a far greater danger to their survival.

HABITAT DESTRUCTION
About two-thirds of the world's birds are threatened by people draining wetlands, cutting down forests, and ploughing up grasslands. More areas could be set aside as bird sanctuaries.

POLLUTION
Oil slicks at sea, acid rain falling on forests or lakes, the use of pesticides on farmland – all this pollution threatens birds. The planet would be a healthier place if pollution was reduced.

HUNTING AND COLLECTING
Hunting birds for food or feathers, or collecting their eggs, has reduced the numbers considerably. We could help birds by banning the hunting of rare species and migrating birds.

INTRODUCED SPECIES
People have often introduced animals such as cats, rats, and mongooses into places they visited or settled. These introduced species compete with native birds and hunt them.

BIRD TRADE
Many people keep birds and songbirds in cages as pets. Some are taken from the wild, and many die in transit because they are tightly packed in small crates and boxes with no food or water.

ISLAND BIRDS
Many rare birds are found only on certain islands, such as the Galapagos, Hawaiian islands or Madagascar. They are especially threatened because their numbers are so low.

NAME	HABITAT	REASON FOR EXTINCTION
HYACINTH MACAW	Brazil, Paraguay, and Bolivia	
DALMATION PELICAN	S.E. Europe, Iran, Turkey, and Russian Federation	
KAKAPO	New Zealand	
WHOOPING CRANE	North America	
ESKIMO CURLEW	North and South America	
IVORY-BILLED WOODPECKER	Cuba, southeastern U.S.A.	
GURNEY'S PITTA	Southern Burma and peninsular Thailand	
NOISY SCRUB BIRD	Western Australia	
WHITE-TAILED SEA EAGLE	Europe	
JAPANESE CRESTED IBIS	Japan and eastern China	
MAURITIUS KESTREL	Mauritius	
KAGU	New Caledonia	
BLACK PARADISE FLYCATCHER	Seychelles	
MONKEY-EATING EAGLE	Philippines	
JUNIN FLIGHTLESS GREBE	South America and Peruvian Andes	

BIRD RECORDS

BIRDS HAVE DEVELOPED some remarkable adaptations of size, movement, appearance, and nesting behaviour. The following examples are some of the more amazing record-breakers.

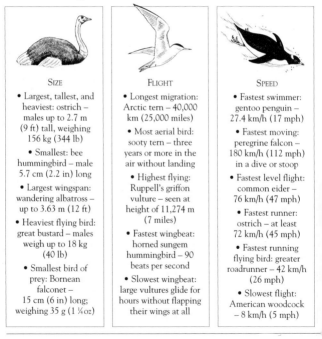

SIZE

- Largest, tallest, and heaviest: ostrich – males up to 2.7 m (9 ft) tall, weighing 156 kg (344 lb)
- Smallest: bee hummingbird – male 5.7 cm (2.2 in) long
- Largest wingspan: wandering albatross – up to 3.63 m (12 ft)
- Heaviest flying bird: great bustard – males weigh up to 18 kg (40 lb)
- Smallest bird of prey: Bornean falconet – 15 cm (6 in) long; weighing 35 g (1 ¼ oz)

FLIGHT

- Longest migration: Arctic tern – 40,000 km (25,000 miles)
- Most aerial bird: sooty tern – three years or more in the air without landing
- Highest flying: Ruppell's griffon vulture – seen at height of 11,274 m (7 miles)
- Fastest wingbeat: horned sungem hummingbird – 90 beats per second
- Slowest wingbeat: large vultures glide for hours without flapping their wings at all

SPEED

- Fastest swimmer: gentoo penguin – 27.4 km/h (17 mph)
- Fastest moving: peregrine falcon – 180 km/h (112 mph) in a dive or stoop
- Fastest level flight: common eider – 76 km/h (47 mph)
- Fastest runner: ostrich – at least 72 km/h (45 mph)
- Fastest running flying bird: greater roadrunner – 42 km/h (26 mph)
- Slowest flight: American woodcock – 8 km/h (5 mph)

FEATHERS

- Fewest: hummingbirds – less than 1,000

- Most: swans – more than 25,000

- Longest: quetzal's tail feather is more than twice the length of its body

NESTS

- Most intricate: African weaver birds

- Largest tree nest: bald eagle – width 2.9 m (9 ½ ft); depth 6 m (19 ½ ft)

- Smallest nest: bee hummingbird – thimble-sized

- Largest communal nest: sociable weaver – up to 300 nest chambers

EGGS

- Smallest: bee hummingbird – 6.35 mm (¼ in) long

- Biggest: ostrich – up to 17.8 cm (7 in) long

- Largest clutch: grey partridge – 15-19 eggs

- Incubation: wandering albatross – 75-82 days

BILLS

- Longest: Australian pelican – 47 cm (1½ft)

- Longest bill compared to body length: sword-billed hummingbird – 10.2 cm (4 in)

- Broadest: shoebill or whale-headed stork – width 12 cm (5 in)

- Sideways curving: wrybill of New Zealand

LIFESPAN

- About 75% of wild birds, such as robins, live less than a year

- Longest-lived ringed seabird: royal albatross – 60 plus

- Oldest captive bird: sulphur-crested cockatoo – 80 plus

SONG

- Most talkative: African grey parrot "Prudle" – 800 words

- Best mimic: marsh warbler – can copy songs of 60 or more other birds

- Loudest: male three-wattled bellbird and the kakapo – calls carry for 1 km (0.6 miles)

Resources

ENGLAND

**The Royal Society for
the Protection of Birds
(RSPB)**
Headquarters and the
Young Ornithologists'
Club (YOC)
The Lodge, Sandy,
Bedfordshire, SG19 2DL
Tel: 0767 680551

**The British Trust for
Ornithology (BTO)**
The Nunnery,
Nunnery Place,
Thetford IP24 2PU
Tel: 0842 750050

**Zoological Society of
London**
Regent's Park,
London NW1 4RY
Tel: 071 722 3333

Hawk and Owl Trust
c/o Birds of Prey Section,
Zoological Society of
London, Regent's Park,
London NW1 4RY

**The Wildfowl and
Wetlands Trust**
Slimbridge,
Gloucestershire GL2 7BT
Tel: 0453 890333

**Birdlife International
(ICBP)**
Wellbrook Court,
Girton Road, Cambridge
CB3 ON
Tel: 0223 277318

**The Natural History
Museum**
Department of
Ornithology, Tring,
Hertfordshire HP23 6AP
Tel: 0442 824181

**Worldwide Fund for
Nature (WWF)** and **Go
Wild!** (a club for young
people aged 7-15)
Panda House, Godalming,
Surrey GU7 1XR
Tel: 0483 426444

**Royal Society for
Nature Conservation
(RSNC)** and junior club
WATCH – information
on county wildlife
The Green, Witham
Park, Waterside South,
Lincoln LN5 7JR
Tel: 0522 544400

The National Trust
36 Queen Anne's Gate,
London SW1H 9AS
Tel: 071 222 9251

**The British Naturalists'
Association**
9/11 Woodfield Road,
London W9 2BA
Tel: 071 435 8782

Birdworld
Holt Pound, Nr
Farnham, Surrey
Tel: 0420 22140

**Field Studies Council
(FSC)** runs wildlife
courses
Montford Bridge,
Shrewsbury SY4 1HW
Tel: 0743 850674

**Fauna and Flora
Preservation Society
(FFPS)**
1 Kensington Gore,
London SW7 2AR
Tel: 071 823 8899

Flimwell Bird Park
Flimwell, Wadhurst,
East Sussex
Tel: 0825 840573

**Bentley Wildfowl
Reserve**
Halland, Nr Lewes,
East Sussex
Tel: 0825 840573

Abbotsbury Swannery
Abbotsbury, Nr
Dorchester, Dorset

English Nature
Headquarters
Northminster House,
Peterborough PE1 1UA
Tel: 0733 340345

SCOTLAND

**RSPB Scottish
Headquarters**
17 Regent Terrace,
Edinburgh EH7 5BN
Tel: 031 557 3136

**The Scottish
Ornithologists' Club**
21 Regent Terrace,
Edinburgh EH7 5BT

WALES

RSPB Wales Office
Bryn Aderyn,
The Bank, Newtown,
Powys SY16 2AB
Tel: 0686 626678

IRELAND

**RSPB Northern Ireland
Office**
Belvoir Forest Park,
Belfast BT8 4QT
Tel: 0232 491547

SOME PLACES TO
WATCH BIRDS:

Arne, Dorset (RSPB)

Bardsey Island,
Gwynedd (Bardsey
Trust)

Bass Rock, Lothian
(Private Reserve,
Scottish Ornithologists'
club)

Bempton Cliffs,
Humberside (RSPB)

Cley Marshes, Norfolk
(Norfolk Naturalists's
Trust)

Cors Tregaron, Dyfed
(National Nature
Reserve)

Dungeness, Kent
(RSPB)

Elmley Marshes, Kent
(RSPB)

Exe Estuary, Devon
Fair Isle, Shetland
(National Trust for
Scotland)

Farne Islands,
Northumberland
(National Trust)

Fetlar, Shetland
(National Trust for
Scotland)

Gower Coast, West
Glamorgan (National
Nature Reserve)

Havergate Island,
Suffolk (RSPB)

Langstone Harbour,
Hampshire (RSPB)

Leighton Moss,
Lancashire (RSPB)

Loch Garten, Highland
(RSPB)

Minsmere, Suffolk
(RSPB)

Morecambe Bay
Lancashire (RSPB)

Ouse Washes,
Cambridgeshire (RSPB,
Wildfowl Trust,
Cambridgeshire
Naturalists' Trust)

Rhum, Highland
(National Nature
Reserve)

Skomer, Dyfed (National
Nature Reserve)

Snettisham, Norfolk
(RSPB)

Stodmarsh, Kent
(National Nature
Reserve)

Strangford Lough,
southern Ireland

Titchwell,
Norfolk (RSPB)

Wicken Fen,
Cambridgeshire
(National Trust)

Glossary

ACID RAIN
Rain that has more acid than normal because of the chemicals from cars, power stations, and factories dissolved in it.

ADAPTATION
Evolutionary process by which living things become fitted to their environment.

AEROFOIL
A wing that is curved on top and flat underneath.

ALTRICIAL
Helpless, blind young birds, with few feathers, which stay in a nest, and rely on their parents for food and warmth.

BARB
Branch from the central shaft of a feather.

BARBULE
Branch from the barb of a feather with tiny hooks along it.

BIRD OF PREY
Common name given to birds that hunt and kill other animals for food. They have hooked bills, talons, and keen senses.

BINOCULAR VISION
Seeing and focussing with both eyes at once.

BROOD PATCH
Featherless area of thickened skin on the underside of a bird's body, used to keep eggs warm during incubation.

CAMOUFLAGE
Colours, markings, or patterns which help living things blend in with their surroundings.

CASQUE
Bony extension of the top part of the bill.

CLUTCH
Set of eggs laid by one female and incubated together.

COLONY
Large number of birds which gather together to breed or roost.

COURTSHIP
Ritual display that takes place before mating.

COVERTS
Groups of small feathers that cover the base of major flight feathers.

CREPUSCULAR
Active at dusk.

CROP
Sac-like extension of a bird's gut used to store food; often used to carry food back to the nest.

DIGESTION
The process by which food is broken down so it can be absorbed into the cells that make up living things

DIURNAL
Active during daylight.

DOWN
Very soft, fine feathers which help to trap air and keep a bird warm.

EGG TOOTH
Structure on the tip of the upper bill with which a chick cracks open the eggshell on hatching.

EXTINCTION
The process by which living things die out of existence.

FLIGHT FEATHERS
Large feathers which make up the wings and can be divided into primary (on the outer wing) and secondary (on the inner wing)

FOLLICLE
Cavity in a bird's skin out of which a feather grows.

GIZZARD
Muscular chamber in the stomach where food is ground up.

INCUBATION
Act of sitting on eggs to keep them warm.

INVERTEBRATE
Animal without a backbone.

IRIDESCENCE
Changing colour with position; colours often shiny like a rainbow.

KERATIN
Protein from which feathers are formed.

LIFT
The force of air that keeps things airborne.

MIGRATION
The movement of animals from one area to another at certain times of the year to find food and warmer climates.

MONOCULAR VISION
Seeing separately with each eye.

MOULTING
The process of shedding old feathers and growing new replacement ones.

NECTAR
Sugary liquid produced by flowers and some leaves to attract some birds for pollination.

NOCTURNAL
Active at night.

PELLET
A hard lump of indigestible pieces of food which some birds, such as owls, cough up.

PIGMENT
A substance that gives colour to eggs and feathers.

PLUMAGE
A bird's feathers.

PRECOCIAL
Down-covered young birds which have their eyes open, and leave the nest soon after hatching.

PREDATOR
An animal which kills other animals for food.

PREENING
Method by which birds care for their feathers using the bill and oil from the preen gland.

POLLINATION
The transfer of pollen from the male to the female parts of flowers or cones so that seeds can develop.

RESPIRATION
The process by which living things release energy from their food.

ROOSTING
Sleeping, including resting behaviour when birds are not actually asleep.

SPECIES
A group of similar birds that can breed together to produce fertile young.

SYRINX
Sound-producing organ in birds, situated where the windpipe joins the tubes leading to the lungs.

TALONS
Sharp, curved claws of birds of prey.

TENDON
Band or cord of tough tissue connecting a muscle with a moveable structure such as a bone.

TERRITORY
Area which a particular bird occupies and defends against other birds of the same species.

THERMAL
Rising column of warm air, used by soaring birds for extra lift.

Species index

Index

Acknowledgements

Dorling Kindersley would like to thank:
Hilary Bird for the index.

Photographs by:
Dennis Avon, Simon Battensby, Jane Burton, Peter Chadwick, Philip Dowell, Mike Dunning, Neil Fletcher, Frank Greenaway, Steve Gorton, Dave King, Colin Keates, Cyril Laubscher, Nick Parfit, Karl Shone, Kim Taylor, Harry Taylor, Jerry Young

Illustrations by:
Angelika Elsebach, Mark Iley, Richard Orr, Maurice Pledger, Colin Salmon, Kevin Toy, John Woodcock

Picture credits: t = top b = bottom c = centre l = left r = right
Dennis Avon 38b, 81bl;110bl. Bruce Coleman 28c;/Jen and Des Bartlett 31 tl;/John Cancalosi106bl;/Patrick Clement 134-135;/Dr. M. T. Kahl 108tr;/Cyril Laubscher 42br;/Gordon Langsbury 120-121b;121r;/Jan van de Kam 100br;/ Luiz Claudio Mango 61tr; George Mcarthy 89b;117tl;/Rinie van Meurs 100 tr;/Bruce Nielson 143tr;/ Charlie Off 90bl;/Hans Reinhard 118cl;129b; 133bc; /Hector Rivarola 113bl;/ Kim Taylor 59b;69cl.
Frank Lane Picture Agency/ E&D Hosking33t;57tr;121tl;130-131;133cr;/ T&P Gardner;/F.Polking 58br;/ Silvestris 88tr;/Roger Tidma 119t;/ Roger Wimshurst 61tr;/ W.Wisniewski 127br. Robert Harding 52cl;53cr;54-55;56cr; 96-97;119b. NHPA /Melvin Grey 23cl; /Peter Johnson 130 bl;/ Peter Parks 34tr;/ Philippa Scott 53tl; 86-87;/John Shaw 53br;112r;114-115. Nature Photographers 41tr;/ E.Lemon 52br;124-125;/H. Miles 126bl;/Paul Sterry 99br;103r;/Derek Washington 64-65;99br. Oxford Scientific Films/ Doug Allen 132l. Papilio 48br;/Larus Argentatus 26-27;53bl; 76-77. Planet Earth Pictures/ Sean Avery 54bl;104-105;/John Eastcott10-11;/ Andre Barttschi 79 bc;/John Lythgou 62b;111tr;/Mark Mattock 98cl;/Yuri Shibbnev 67tl. Kim Taylor 24-25b; 56cr.

Every effort has been made to trace the copyright holders and we apologise in advance for any unintentional omissions. We would be pleased to insert the appropriate acknowledgement in any subsequent edition of this publication.